PLAY CULTURE IN A CHANGING WORLD

This book, based on a larger academic version (commissioned by Tuomas Seppa), 'Angelprincess and Suicide on the Playground Slide: The Culture of Play and Societal Change', was first published in Finnish by Gaudeamus, 1999.

Series Editor: Tina Bruce

The intention behind the 'Debating Play' series is to encourage readers to reflect on their practices so that they are in a position to offer high quality play opportunities to children. The series will help those working with young children and their families in diverse ways and contexts, to think about how to cultivate early childhood play with rich learning potential.

The 'Debating Play' series examines cultural myths and taboos. It considers matters of human rights and progress towards inclusion in the right to play for children with complex needs. It looks at time-honoured practices and argues for the removal of constraints on emergent play. It challenges readers to be committed to promoting play opportunities for children traumatized by war, flight, violence and separation from loved ones. The series draws upon crucial con-temporary research which demonstrates how children in different parts of the world develop their own play culture in ways which help them make sense of their lives.

Published and forthcoming titles in the 'Debating Play' series, edited by Tina Bruce:

Forbes: *Beginning to Play*
Holland: *We Don't Play With Guns Here*
Hyder: *War, Conflict and Play*
Manning-Morton and Thorp: *Key Times for Play*
Orr: *My Right to Play: A Child with Complex Needs*

PLAY CULTURE IN A CHANGING WORLD

Marjatta Kalliala

Open University Press

Open University Press
McGraw-Hill Education
McGraw-Hill House
Shoppenhangers Road
Maidenhead
Berkshire
England
SL6 2QL

email: enquiries@openup.co.uk
world wide web: www.openup.co.uk

and Two Penn Plaza, New York, NY 10121-2289, USA

First published 2006

A catalogue record of this book is available from the British Library

ISBN-13: 978 0335 21341 2 (pb)   978 0335 21342 9 (hb)
ISBN-10: 0 335 213413 (pb)   0 335 21342 1 (hb)

Library of Congress Cataloging-in-Publication Data
CIP data applied for

Typeset by RefineCatch Limited, Bungay, Suffolk
Printed in the UK by Bell & Bain Ltd, Glasgow

CONTENTS

Series Editor's Preface   vii
Acknowledgements   x
Introduction: A picture of children's play culture   1

1   **Meet the children, their parents, and the practitioners who work with them**   3

2   **In general: The changing world we live in**   10

3   **From the general to the particular: What is children's play culture?**   17

4   **Competitions and games in children's play culture**   30

5   **Games of chance and luck in children's play culture: *Alea***   43

6   **The world of make-believe 1: Family play scenarios**   51

7   **The world of make-believe 2: Play scenarios that are about having 'adventures' and fights**   75

8   **Fooling about in play: The 'dizzy' side of play culture**   94

9   Play that defies categorization   106

10   Gender and children's play culture   108

11   Adults and play   117

12   Changes in children's play culture   132

Appendix: Interviews   141
References   143
Index   151

SERIES EDITOR'S PREFACE

When I invited Marjatta Kalliala, who works in the Early Childhood Studies department of the University of Helsinki, to write a book in the 'Debating Play' Series, I was delighted when she accepted. I think we both knew intuitively that we were undertaking something that required a pioneering spirit. There are many cooperative ventures between colleagues in different countries, but usually these are between people who share (or almost share) the same language, such as those English speakers and writers working in the UK, the USA, Australia, Canada and New Zealand. The challenge for me and for Marjatta has been to put into accessible English her work on children's play culture.

Pioneering is never easy, and this book has taken time. But we have both learnt so much as it has taken shape. I have been fascinated and challenged by her work on the importance of children's play culture. I have experienced something which I knew intellectually, and theoretically, but had never had the excitement of being involved in so deeply, that translation from one language to another is not a simple thing. Language really does express culture and ideas in the deepest and often different ways. Marjatta's English is good, and my Finnish is non-existent, but we have worked hard to turn her text into one which is relevant and meaningful for English-speaking readers, who have not experienced Finnish culture. The result is a book which helps our understanding of some of the essentials of play, wherever it is found.

I wanted to see this book published because it gave me the same kind of excitement that I had experienced when first reading four authors on early education theories. They span different times and different cultures:

Susan Isaacs in the 1930s – UK

Intellectual Growth in Young Children (1930), London: Routledge and Kegan Paul.

Social Development in Young Children: A Study of Beginnings (1933), London: Routledge and Kegan Paul.

John Gabriel Navarra in the 1950s – USA

The Development of Scientific Concepts in a Young Child: A Case Study (1955), New York: Teachers College.

Vivian Gussin Paley in the 1980s/1990s – USA

Wally's Stories (1981), Cambridge, MA: Harvard University Press.

Mollie Is Three: Growing Up in School (1986), Chicago: University of Chicago Press.

The Boy Who Would Be a Helicopter (1990), Cambridge, MA: Harvard University Press.

John Matthews in the 1980s – UK

Drawing and Painting: Children and Visual Representation (2003, 2nd edn) London: Paul Chapman Publishing Ltd.

These books are all based on informed, and ethically researched, observations of children. They all give us further insights and understanding of children, and each in a different way deepens the way we take forward our practice, supporting and developing children's ideas, and our affection and respect for children. They all help us to develop our practice, but only if we tune into the way children think, and if we continue learning ourselves.

This book, by Marjatta Kalliala, resonates with the way that Susan Isaacs showed us the darker side of children's play, but also their sexuality and need to be 'dizzy' and to experience 'whirling water' when developing socially and intellectually. Navarra demonstrated the growth of his son LB's scientific concepts through his play. John Matthews gave us insights into the visual representations of children. In this book, Marjatta shows us the play culture young children need to develop for themselves as they move through their early childhood. Her work shows us (as Vivian Gussin Paley does, in an entirely different way), the worries, fears and aspirations that children have, and how they deal with life with such courage and intellectual energy.

Earlier books in the 'Debating Play' Series, by Julia Manning-Morton and Maggie Thorp, and by Ruth Forbes have focused on the early emergence of play. This book emphasizes play in the later part of early childhood, and in doing so takes us into children's own play culture.

Above the door of the former Kindergarten Training College in Helsinki, carved in stone, are the words by Froebel, 'Let us live with our children'. When we tune into the hearts and minds of children, and their physically embodied selves, we continue to learn in ways which develop our practice. This book is about doing that in relation to the way children develop their own play culture.

Tina Bruce

ACKNOWLEDGEMENTS

Throughout the process that has led to this book I have carried the children I met in mind. Without them the book would not exist. I learnt most from them. My warm thanks to every one of them for all the information (or maybe simply for everything) that helped me to deepen my understanding of play.

I also want to thank the parents and staff in the three day care settings the children attended. Their contribution was indispensable.

For the original Finnish academic version I owe thanks to Professor Bo Lönnquist for inspiring supervision at the beginning of my work. I thank Professor J. U. E. Lehtonen for encouraging me to work independently and Docent Teppo Korhonen for apposite remarks. I thank Professor Juha Siltala for stimulating discussions and thought provoking seminars. The way he urges people to think made me go further with my work than I would have done otherwise. I also thank Professor Airi Hautamäki for intensive discussions on childhood and the history of the family from past to present.

I thank my colleague and friend Leena Tahkokallio for endless discussions and listening. Her expertise on play has meant an indispensable opportunity to try out ideas against intimate knowledge that has cumulated during tens of years. I also want to thank her for support during the process of making the English version.

In the acknowledgements of the Finnish version I heartily thank Tina Bruce for reflexive discussions that broadened my understanding of the meaning of play. For the English version I owe the greatest deal to her. It has been a long process to work my first English draft version into this book. In this context editing means much more work than it normally does. Language is one thing, cultural differences another. My Fenglish needed to be rewritten and pruned into accessible

English. In addition we had to construct a shared understanding of the 'style' of the book i.e. of what it means to write an accessible book for the English audience.

I warmly thank Tina Bruce for all the work she has undertaken during this process. I am grateful for her patience and resiliency. Without her wise advice and invigorating sense of humour the English version would never have became true.

INTRODUCTION: A PICTURE OF CHILDREN'S PLAY CULTURE

In this book we shall look at children's play culture in a changing world. Chapter 1 is about meeting the children, their parents and practitioners who work with them. The focus is on how to make children's voices heard and their play culture visible.

In order to understand the way that children play, both as individuals and in groups, both in early childhood settings and at home, we need to make a connection with the general cultural climate of the historic era. The changing nature of childhood and adulthood is the focus of Chapter 2, because the way parents and practitioners see children and understand their life today impacts on children's play culture in far-reaching ways.

In Chapter 3, we look at play as phenomenon, adults' understandings of play and Roger Caillois' classification of play (1961). In fact, Caillois wasn't interested in children's play *per se*. He was interested in play as a phenomenon. But his work proved to be invaluable because it covered exceptionally well the material on play that was gathered through talking to children about their playing and through observing them. This leads us to tackle the question, what do we mean by children's play culture? We shall see that children's play culture is not the same as child culture, which is adult-led, and created by adults for children.

In Chapters 4–9 we shall give voice to the children we have met. These chapters are based on observations and interviews of children. In Chapter 4, we turn our attention to the way that competition and games with rules form an important strand in children's play culture. Traditionally this has been the focus of the studies of folklore researchers, such as the Opies in the UK (Opie and Opie 1959, 1985). We shall also see how these games are dependent on the changes that have taken place in Western societies, including Finland and the UK, in the past decades. Chapter 5 shows how children value games of chance and destiny, which is closely linked to Chapter 4.

In Chapter 6 we look at the world of make-believe. First, we explore games of make-believe that are inspired by human relationships, especially that of mother and child, man and woman. Here we see the persistence of fundamental play themes alongside new variations of old themes that emerge with the pace of changes in family life and the media environment.

Chapter 7 explores the world of make-believe in its other dimensions. There are play scenarios about having 'adventures' and fights between good and evil guys. Here we see how children use what they have seen and heard to create new versions of narratives that belong to their shared cultural competence. Children's own ideas of their playing help adults understand how meaningful these play experiences are for children.

Chapter 8 introduces an area of children's play culture which is usually ignored, and does not often feature in books on play in the UK, although it was touched on by Susan Isaacs in the 1930s. It is described as the 'dizzy' side of play, and involves children fooling about. This kind of playing is universal and to a certain extent independent of cultural factors. Adults, early childhood practitioners and parents alike, do not warm to this kind of play, especially in today's world. However, both children and brain researchers have something to say about this kind of play.

In Chapter 9 play that defies categorization is mentioned. In Chapter 10 the issues of gender are examined. These recur throughout the book, but are given particular focus in this chapter. We hear what children themselves think about gender play. This raises important issues for those practitioners working in the UK, since by the age of 6, children are at school and have less opportunity to develop their play in mixed age groups, or single gender groups.

Chapter 11 gives attention to the relationship between adults and children, and how this impacts on children's play culture nowadays. Again, there are some uncomfortable messages which need to be addressed by practitioners.

In the last chapter, we take a look into the future, and the need for encouragement and actions which promote rich environments in which children at least up to 7 years of age can develop their play culture.

This book presents a challenging picture of children's play culture in our changing world, and will provide a useful guide to future practice directions.

1

MEET THE CHILDREN, THEIR PARENTS, AND THE PRACTITIONERS WHO WORK WITH THEM

In this chapter, we shall look at the importance of:

- talking to children and listening to what they tell us about their play culture;
- observing their play;
- finding out what parents and practitioners know and understand about children's play culture.

We shall meet the children first, and then their parents and the practitioners who work with them. With the help of the practitioners working with the children, I sent a letter to the parents of the 6-year-old children in three day-care centres in Finland, asking if I could interview them and their children about their play, both in the day-care setting and at home. The material obtained through talking with children and observing them at play is core material, and has influenced this book.

If we want to understand how children's play culture has changed, we need to compare it with an earlier period. The 1950s has been chosen, and despite the lack of comparable material, there are useful documentary resources and contemporary research which can help in this.

The children

The 23 children are all living in Helsinki. They are all aged 6, and have already developed their play culture to quite an extent. It is from their perspective that we shall see what is important to them in the

way they play. In the same way we can see how young children growing up in urban America develop their play in the fascinating books
by Vivian Gussin Paley or in the 1930s we saw the children at the
Malting House School, in Cambridge, with whom Susan Isaacs
worked. Currently the work of Penny Lancaster 2005 (a recent publi-
cation) through the 'Listening to Children' Project based at 'Coram
Family' is in the same spirit.

Adults as insiders and outsiders

An adult meeting the children has to decide what kind of role to
adopt. Harriet Strandell (1994) chose the role of an outsider. She does
not interact with the children or the adults as she does her research
work but remains a distant observer. William Corsaro (1997), on the
other hand, used a 'reactive' method of field entry into children's
world. He enters free play areas, sits down and waits for the children
to react to him. Sooner or later, the children begin to ask him questions, draw him into their activities and gradually define him as an
atypical adult. This is the way he becomes an insider.

How I met the children

For me, the crucial question regarding my role was my relationship
with the children. I tried to get across to the children two things:

1 You know something I do not know.
2 What you know is very important and is very interesting to me.

In this way children were defined as the experts of their own play
culture, and this was to characterize the interaction between us
(Corsaro 1985). This is connected with the view that an adult has to
genuinely accept the children's perspectives. Children have the right
to their own experiences. They have the right to be interested in
matters that adults do not find interesting. They have right to their
own opinions. Without the experience of the right to their own
perspective, it is hard for children to express their own ideas (Eide
1989).
    Before I started the interviews, I developed my cultural competence
through watching videos of *Biker Mice*, *Power Rangers* and *The
Lion King*. Children were delighted when they noticed that I knew the
plot of *Biker Mice* and could tell the united colours of the Power
Rangers.

Children at play tell stories about themselves to themselves ■

Homo ludens, playing man, is at the same time *Homo narrans*, story-telling man. Adapting what Clifford Geertz (1993) says, we can see that children at play tell stories about themselves to themselves. However, play as a narrative is directly understandable only to the players themselves because it is often impossible for an outside observer to grasp the inner pictures that support the playing. When a child jumps down the playground slide, if we only observe this, we are settling for a 'thin description' (Ryle 1971; Geertz 1993). Perhaps the playground slide is a waterfall. If it is, then the interpretation needs to be different, because this is more than just children playing about on a slide.

When children talk about their playing, the information gathered through observation grows and becomes more precise. In this book, narratives about children's play culture are traced and generated mainly through talking with the children and observing them. The advantage of this method is that it allows the children to say what they are playing. It helps us to understand the how and the why of play and we can strive for 'thick description' (Ryle 1971, Geertz 1993).

A mushroom-picking strategy ■

Meeting the children can be compared to mushroom picking. If you want to pick lots, you have to be ready to meander both to the left and right, but at the same time you have to keep the main direction in your mind in order not to become lost. The route previously planned might be good but often you have to find a new one and you always have to be ready to follow small paths pointed out by the children. If you only look for what you have decided to look for earlier, you will find only what you thought you would find and a great deal of delicious and edible mushrooms are left untouched in the forest. It does no harm either if you determine some of the mushrooms only afterwards. Thus, I allowed small deviations and still kept the main theme in my mind.

My interviews with children could be characterized as discussions or chatting rather than asking questions. In fact, my approach corresponded to Reidar Kvale's (1996: 5–6) definition of the aim of semi-structured interviews: 'semi-structured interviews are discussions, the aim of which is to generate interpretable descriptions of the sphere of life of the interviewees'.

I used a *carpe diem* method, i.e., I started chatting (and tape recording) whenever it seemed natural. At the day-care centres it meant that I could start the interview outdoors and finish it inside in a den under the table.

The interviewees defined play for their part while answering the question 'What are you playing?' The discussions around the outskirts of play are necessary because they consolidate the background of play that is important in understanding the foreground.

Talking to parents

The parents were highly motivated in supporting my aim to find out about their children's play culture and were willing to cooperate. My starting point was that parents know their own children best of all and I tried to indicate that there were no wrong answers.

Parents willingly answered even the most demanding questions, but they still defined the topics we discussed. For my part, I tried to avoid leading questions. Active listening is as important as asking. The answers the parents gave signalled the direction they wanted to take. When I followed their clues, new themes emerged, such as their children's relationship to nature. That had not been part of my initial questioning.

The children, with only one exception, were present during the talks with their parents, and they also influenced the discussion. They were not passive listeners but commented on what their parents said about them.

The presence of the children during the interviews reflects the new relationship between adults and children. We see in practice the 'emotional democracy' that Giddens (1994) discusses. Children's comments are not seen by their parents as impertinent but as opinions worth paying attention to. Only one father told his children that he was the one being interviewed and that they were supposed to stay in their room while he was being interviewed. Although parents may have left some things unsaid because the children were present, it does mean that the interview material has passed the censorship of the children.

Talking with the practitioners about the children's play

I met the heads of the day-care centres, the kindergarten teachers and the nursery nurses in three day-care centres. Ulpukka and Kesäkumpu are small inner-city day-care centres. Hilapieli is a large day-care centre in a suburb with its own building and a large playground.

During the group discussions everyone was highly motivated. There was no need to coax anybody to participate. The subject was one that interested them and the discussion proceeded without difficulty. I felt my role was one of a catalyst as the group was already interested in the children's play.

The pros and cons of group discussions

Group interviews are often both criticized and defended using the same arguments. The staff sometimes soften their opinions in the direction of the views generally accepted by the group. They might not at other times, therefore, bring their personal ideas to the discussion as strongly as in an individual interview. This can be taken as an advantage or disadvantage depending on the situation. If the aim is to sketch the general orientation that guides the play culture of the day-care centres, the compromise of the group discussions is more interesting and useful than the more nuanced and unpolished picture obtained through individual interviews. The consensus of the day-care centres is put together through these general opinions and areas of genuine accordance. Extreme points of view are avoided in Finnish day-care centres which are very democratic. 'The culture of accordance' is very strong.

The observations

Through observation it is possible to grasp children's authentic playing. This is because it has not been changed into words about play. The processes of play, its complexity and the contradictory forces of unification and dissolution are visible only in play. My attempt to find out about children's play culture worked best when I was able to combine my observations with children's talk about their play. Confidence is necessary for observation. My presence did not seem to bother the children even when their playing became wild and touched the boundaries of what was allowed.

When I observed the children at play, I mostly wrote notes by hand. When possible, I also used the tape recorder in order to record authentic dialogues. On one occasion the children incorporated the tape-recorder into their play.

An essential part of successful field work is the dialogue with the children and the adults, with oneself, the material and other researchers. The most important thing when observing children at play, and when talking to children about their play is the relationship you have with them. When the relationship is good, the discussion is rich and helps adults to listen and understand children's play.

After having met the children ⬛

After the mushroom picking you have to decide what to do with the miscellaneous pile of mushrooms – or with the material consisting of tape-recorded interviews and observation notes. The transcription of the recoding tapes reveals what you have picked. At first sight there seems to be too many sorts of mushroom, and too much of everything. The challenge is how to sort them out.

When I started to sort out my pile I found that the understanding children have about their play was vast. Because I wanted to respect the children's understanding of play I left the difficult definition of play to the children themselves. When children answered my question 'What are you playing at?', they also implicitly, and without realizing it, defined what play is. This also meant that I found answers to the question: 'What do children play today?'

I also found that the classification of play which matched most comfortably the material gathered with children was that of Roger Caillois (1961). Thus, tape recordings of the discussions of the children, the parents and the staff were analysed using Caillois' classification of play which consists of four types of play: competition, chance and destiny, imitation and dizziness. His work was translated into English in 1961. He is interested in play as a phenomenon, and his classification of play helps us understand that different kinds of play appeal to different sides of children. It is invaluable for early childhood practitioners to understand that one kind of play does not compensate for another kind of play. Instead, a full variation of play is needed for full satisfaction.

In addition to this I sorted out what the children and the adults said about gender play, how staff at the day-care centres defined their role in relation to play, and what parents thought was important for their children's play.

In this chapter we have seen the importance of listening to the children, the parents and the practitioners and looked at effective ways of finding out about the children's play culture.

Questions for reflective practice ⬛

• How do you observe the play of children you work with?

- What techniques in this chapter will help you to develop and inform your observations of children at play?
- What techniques in the chapter will help ensure that you tune into how parents see their children's play?

Further reading

Corsaro, W. (1985) *Friendship and Peer Culture in the Early Years.* Norwood, N J: Ablex.

Gussin-Paley, V. G. (1984) *Boys and Girls: Superheroes in the Doll Corner.* Chicago: University of Chicago Press.

Lancaster, P. (2005) *Listening to Children.* London: Open University Press.

2

IN GENERAL: THE CHANGING WORLD WE LIVE IN

In this chapter, we shall look at some aspects of general culture which are universal and the way that children's play culture exists as part of this general cultural scene. This means that this chapter is about the two outer circles in Figure 2.1. In Chapter 3 we shall explore the inner circle.

The changes that we are seeing in society as a whole are impacting on adults' and children's lives. At first glance, we do not realize that some of these changes deeply influence the way children play. This is because most of the changes do not influence children's play culture directly but indirectly. Some examples of the changes influencing children's play culture are:

- how people earn a living;
- urbanization;
- more middle-aged and elderly people in the population;
- the increasing equality of women;
- the changing work patterns of women outside the home;
- changing class boundaries and social stratification;
- changing professions;
- changing sexual behaviour;
- changes in the nuclear family and childhood;
- no clear common ideology, religious movements or doctrines to give cohesion and shared understandings;
- changing institutions (e.g. church and state);
- changes in the welfare state and thinking what's best for society.

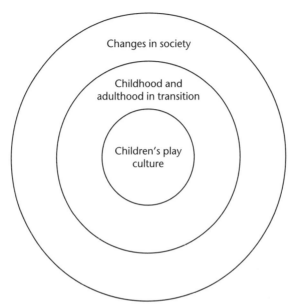

Figure 2.1 Fundamental cultural changes impacting on children's play culture

Disorder and discontinuity in the world of today

The period from the seventeenth to the end of the twentieth century is usually described as 'modern'. It was characterized by universal values, continuity and a sense of progress being made. Now children are growing up with different influences affecting their childhood, which is often described as 'postmodern'. This rejects the 'modern' idea that there are universally shared values, or that there is continuity with progress resulting.

Some people, like Thomas Ziehe (1982), believe that freedom from the old traditions brings enrichment and offers possibilities. They would say that it is no longer necessary to conform, or remain the same for the whole of our lives. Instead, we can try out different identities, and change. Having an individual sense of identity is central to living in the western world today.

However, this also means that individuals face heavier demands than before. According to Ulrich Beck (1994), everybody has the freedom and the need to act, stage, play and direct his or her own biography, identity, social networks, commitments and convictions.

Childhood and adulthood in transition ■

The general changes in society influence parenthood and childhood as well. The influence of the changing roles of parents is seen in the everyday life of children in many ways and naturally also in the way children play.

From certain to uncertain parenting

In the past, parents bringing up children with the ideal that their children will internalize the commonly shared values did not question their authority as parents. They felt comfortable about transferring their values to their children and setting firm boundaries for them. Parents also set a firm boundary between 'play' and 'not play'. Children had to behave well at the table but they also had a great deal of freedom to play, especially outdoors.

Parents today are less certain and more permissive. Instead of values, they emphasize social skills and individual competencies. At the same time increasingly, they tend to move the responsibility of child rearing away from the family, so that the role of professionals and specialists is becoming more central than ever before (Beck-Gernsheim 1992).

In principle, permissive adults are permissive also towards play. They want to give more freedom to the children than before, but, on the other hand, a society burdened with environmental threats and other dangers sets new boundaries for children. For example, parents today often feel guilty and helpless about allowing their children the sort of freedom that was part of their own childhood earlier because of the following:

- restrictions caused by traffic;
- pollution;
- age segregation in group settings of all kinds;
- the need to provide safe places to play which means children are fenced off and separated from the wider world.

The impact of institutionalization ■

- *1950s – The 'stressed' child in group day-care.* In the 1950s, to have a full-time place in day-care was seen as negative and stigmatizing. Long days were considered stressful for young children, and full-time groups were avoided whenever possible.

- *Towards the 'competent' child in group day-care.* From the 1970s, more and more full-time provision became available for families as more mothers worked outside the home. The view of the 'stressed child' needed to change. Eeva Hujala (1998) states that the situation required the vision of a competent child, able to adapt in the day-care centre without the anxiety that the 'emotional' child experienced (1998).
- *Today – The 'child's individual right to full-time provision' in group day-care.* Since the 1990s the poor full-time children separated from their parents have become 'clients' of day-care. In Finland, it is not the parents' or the family's right, but the right of an individual child to receive day-care services.

How adults interact with and relate to children

The relationship between adults and children has changed in western countries nowadays. Finland and the UK are no exception but in Finland the changes are particularly obvious. This is shown in the following ways:

- emphasis on becoming independent early;
- the development of 'pal' parenthood;
- emotional democracy.

Encouraging children to become independent early

The dependence and neediness of a child are seen as a problem. Adults want children to take responsibility for their decisions and their consequences much sooner than before. Parents may be friends, pals, confidants or advisers but they can also leave their children more or less without guidance or contact with adults (Hoikkala 1993).

'Pal' parenthood

If the relationship of parents to their children is more as a 'pal' than one of guidance and education as in the past, we can no longer talk of 'bringing up' children, or 'child rearing'. Instead, we begin to talk about ways of relating and interacting between family members of different ages. Authoritarian parents (especially fathers) disappear altogether (Hoikkala 1993).

Emotional democracy

Anthony Giddens (1994) talks about the 'emotional democracy' that emerges in relationships between parents and children. Hierarchical orders of relationships are rejected and parents appeal to children through discussion, and are taught to choose for themselves between alternatives. Through negotiation, parents try to educate their children to become socially flexible and co-operative but there is also a move towards the idea of self-education (Björnberg 1992; Hoikkala 1993; Frönes 1994).

Contrasting images of the child

The 'marginalized' child

If the vulnerability and neediness, strong emotions and complicated ways of thinking of young children are emphasized, it can be argued that this makes a pathology of childhood which stresses the differences between children and adults. It under-estimates children, presenting them as immature, irrational, incompetent, asocial and acultural, while adults are seen as mature, rational, competent, social and independent (Alanen 1992; Strandell 1994). According to this view of children, they are, on the one hand, excluded from society and treated as dependent, but, on the other, given special treatment.

The 'competent' child

This conception is based on seeing children as:

• active social agents who construct and create for themselves their social relationships;
• subjects and citizens who produce new knowledge.

The active, creative, social and skilful side of children is emphasized and children's needs are primarily seen as culturally dependent and socially constructed not innate and universal (Kitzinger 1990; Prout and James 1990; Strandell 1994).

These contrasting images of childhood easily result in disputes and an either–or situation which prevent the many-sided examination of the complex changes of childhood. For example, if we think about play, which is the special interest of this book, it can be seen both as something innate and as a culturally dependent phenomenon.

Ideal models of child-rearing practices for the good of the child ∎

While the child of the 1950s faced the risk of being restricted by unambiguous rules, the child today might suffer insecurity because there are no clear rules. In Finland, Airi Hautamäki and Lea Pulkkinen have outlined what they describe as *authoritative parenthood*. They combine the best aspects of certain and uncertain child-rearing practices. Parents are both demanding and rigorous and understanding and loving.

The vital family, formulated by David Elkind (1994), consists of the same kind of elements. The vitality of the family depends on to what extent it nourishes the needs, talents and opportunities of both children and parents. In other words, Elkind combines the best elements of the modern *nuclear family* and the postmodern *permeable family* to create the ideal of a vital family. Elkind challenges individual parents to regain their lost adulthood, although he admits that the changes in the family are dependent on societal changes.

Real life always resists theoretical and simplified models, but the signs of change are clear. Although a child is always dependent on adults in many ways and cannot do without their care and protection, the consequences of this fact are contradictory. The crisis of modernity means the end of clear boundaries between adulthood and childhood. This also influences children's play culture. In the chapters that follow we will face this and find some ways forward in an increasingly complex world.

Questions for reflective practice ∎

- Reflect on the families you work with. Are the children experiencing certain, uncertain or 'vital' parenting?
- Discuss the importance of agreed values with someone who brought up children in the 1950s and someone bringing up children now. Compare their perspectives on childhood play and parenting.

Futher reading ∎

Elkind, D. (1994) *Ties That Stress: The New Family Imbalance.* Cambridge, MA: Harvard University Press.

Hautamäki, A. (2000) The matrix of relationships in the late modern family in the Nordic countries: a heaven in a heartless world, a disturbed nest or a secure base? In A. Hautamäki (ed.) *Emergent*

Trends in Early Childhood Education. Towards an Ecological and Psychohistorical Analysis of Quality. Helsinki: University of Helsinki, Research Report no. 216, pp. 33–107.

Prout, A. and James, A. (eds) (1990) *Constructing and Reconstructing Childhood: Contemporary Issues in the Sociological Study of Childhood*. London: Falmer Press.

3

FROM THE GENERAL TO THE PARTICULAR: WHAT IS CHILDREN'S PLAY CULTURE?

In this chapter we shall first look at play as a phenomenon and answer the question, 'What is play?' Some approaches to play that complement each other and are fruitful from the point of view of the focus of this book are presented. The definition and classification of play by Roger Caillois are of special interest because they correspond to children's own understandings of what play is. In the second part of this chapter we will look at how children construct their play culture.

What is play?

Johan Huizinga (1947), philosopher and cultural historian, argues that *homo ludens*, 'playing man' describes the essential nature of people better than *homo sapiens*, 'wise man'. Play is one of the main categories of human activity. Huizinga tries to show that play is the core element of culture and it is born in the form of play. Roger Caillois shares Huizinga's ideas on the importance of play for culture but he criticizes Huizinga's classification of play, arguing that Huizinga only pays attention to 'higher play', that is, social play that has its origin in two elements:

- fighting for something;
- playing roles.

Because Huizinga emphasizes the 'useful' aspects of play, he ignores the 'useless' and chaotic elements of play. The definition and classification of play by Caillois (1961) are of great interest in this book, because he looks at both the 'higher' and the chaotic elements of play.

It is hard to define a phenomenon like play. According to Caillois, play is an activity which might be characterized as:

- voluntary
- detached from ordinary life
- unpredictable
- unproductive
- imaginative
- in accordance with the rules.

Play is voluntary

Like Huizinga, Caillois values the freedom of play and how people take part in it voluntarily. It is not possible to force or even coax somebody to play without losing something essential about the proper essence of play. The pleasure and fascination of play are due to spontaneous and unconscious involvement in it. The extreme absorption of children at play can be described by the concept of 'flow'. Spontaneous joy, delight and inseparability of self, action and environment are typical of the experience of flow (Huizinga 1947; Csikszentmihalyi 1975; Bruce 1991).

Play is detached from ordinary life

Play is detached from ordinary life although the contents of play are often derived from real life. It is important to distinguish play from other kinds of activities. Gregory Bateson (1976) became interested in how players signal to each other the essential message, 'this is play'. The players must understand the paradoxical character of messages of play. For example, a playful bite has to be interpreted as both a bite and 'not a bite', both at the same time. The message 'this is play' is not a single message that precedes play acting. According to Bateson, communication always takes place on several levels and so the message of play always constructs both:

- text (describing the substance of play);
- context (outlining the framework of play).

These two levels, text and context, help children to distinguish play from 'real life'. What Bateson says applies even to young children, because it emphasizes non-verbal as well as verbal playful gestures, smiles and laughter as play signals as well as what the children say.

It is important to understand the message 'this is play' because play is not so much activities of a certain kind but is, rather, an attitude. Jumping, throwing a stone, seizing another person, even asking questions or imitating another person's speech may or may not be play (Garvey 1977). In fantasy play, pretending is the element that makes play-acting detached from real life.

Play is unpredictable

Having a predictable and inevitable end result, without any surprises is against the very nature of play. The game is spoiled if the winner is known in advance. In fantasy play, there need to be possibilities for spontaneous inventions and changes.

Play is unproductive

According to Caillois and others, play has no products. It does not bring success, property or anything new. When it is over, the players are the same as they were before. Nevertheless, researchers often emphasize learning through play so strongly that play is primarily examined from the perspective of a child's development and learning.

Bateson (1955) uses the concept of *deuterolearning* to describe the process of learning to learn which is as multi-layered as play. According to Bateson, it is through play acting that children learn a new viewpoint and understand something about the different contexts.

Play is imaginative

For Jean Piaget (1972), play is an indication of a child's level of thinking. For him, symbolic play means intellectual immaturity compared with, for example, games with rules.

Lev Vygotsky (1976), for his part, objects to examining play to indicate children's level of cognitive development because, it leads to looking at playing children 'as incompetent mathematicians who are not yet able to write symbols on paper and therefore describe their thinking through action'.

According to Vygotsky, when children play, they operate at the highest level possible, in 'the zone of proximal development'. This corresponds with their next developmental level, the level of performance that they are able to reach, in other kinds of activities, only with the help of an adult. Vygotsky finds that play is the indispensable precondition for intellectual development, because creating imaginative situations leads to developing abstract thinking. In practice, reaching the level of concrete operations in thinking (Piaget) does not extinguish the fascination of fantasy play. Older children still enjoy fantasy play (Singer and Singer 1992). Children adapt many kinds of skills as they play, so that they can use these essential elements and spontaneously seize the moment for play.

Play is in accordance with the rules

In games with rules, rules correspond to the imaginative element of fantasy play in the sense that it is expressly through rules that the separated space for play is created.

Children don't play in order to learn, although they learn while they are playing

Compared to other researchers, Caillois' criteria of unproductiveness may look strange. As we have seen, both Piaget and Vygotsky emphasize the way that play paves the way for later development and learning. Children seem to learn various skills while playing and generate 'learning products'. One way of interpreting Caillois' emphasis on the idea of unproductiveness is that children's motives in play are not progressive. Children don't play in order to learn although they do learn while they are playing.

Caillois' categories of play

Caillois strives for a classification of play which is as inclusive as possible – and tries to crystallize the essence of different types of play with only a few concepts. According to him, the four main types of play with corresponding themes are:

- competition (*agon*);
- chance (*alea*);
- imitation (*mimicry*);
- dizziness (*ilinx*).

Although Caillois strives for a universal classification, he admits that it is not possible to cover the whole field of play with only four concepts. He gives the example of flying a kite to show what remains outside his classification where the playful nature of the activity is easy to recognize but difficult to define using the concepts competition, chance, imitation and dizziness.

Despite its limitations, the main advantage of Caillois' classification probably lies in the fact that it enables the identification of the different motives that are essential for different types of play. Competition, chance, mimicry and dizziness are perhaps not the first concepts one thinks of when reflecting or different types of play. However, the categories prove to be powerful when the aim is to sketch a general picture of children's play culture.

Competition (*agon*)

The starting point for many games and those with rules is competition. Equal opportunities that are created artificially through rules are characteristics of these games. The motive for competition is winning. Children challenge each other to curious trials before competitions with fixed rules begin. Who can endure tickling the longest? Who can flutter their eyelashes better than the rest? The idea is that you are not allowed to flutter your eyelids. If you do, you lose the game.

Chance and destiny (*alea*)

In this kind of play, it is not the 'best' who wins, but the one who has the best luck. Games of dice, roulette, heads or tails, lottery and lotto are typical examples of *alea*. The fascination of these games is based on the element of chance and haphazardness. In some games, like dominos and most card games, competition and chance are combined. Cards are divided haphazardly but after that the players have the possibility to make the most of their talent.

Imitation (*mimicry*)

Make-believe play demands that the illusion is shared. The players not only experience something in a fantasy world but also change into imagined persons and act according to these roles. They put their soul into their roles and abandon their own personality in order to pretend to be someone else.

Children imitate adults both in earnest and 'as if'. According to Sara

Smilansky (1968), fantasy play promotes imitating socializing because in their play children can excel and create versions of adults' life that are richer than real life. Because there are often two or more players in make-believe play, verbal communication is an essential part of play. In make-believe play children can be seen as actors, but also as scriptwriters, directors and set designers, yet still children (Garvey 1990).

For Susan Isaacs (1929) the decisive meaning of make-believe play for children is that it represents the first step towards the release of meaning from direct 'here and now' perceptions. This enables development of the 'as if' consciousness. The applications of *mimicry* become wider in adult life. Theatre and different kinds of drama interpretations without doubt belong to this group. Today the live role play of young adults is probably one of the adult applications of *mimicry* that comes closest to children's make-believe play.

Dizziness (*ilinx*)

Dizziness is the fourth category of play. The idea is, for a moment, to shake the trustworthiness of perception and sensation, thus creating an enjoyable feeling of dizziness. Every child knows that twirling round makes them feel dizzy. Swinging, falling, sliding and the quickening of rectilinear motion or its combinations with revolving motion generate the feeling of physical vertigo.

Also games with rules may end in dizziness and chaos. Brian Sutton-Smith (1976) has mapped games of order and disorder that are found in both Western and non-Western cultures.

Mental dizziness is parallel to physical dizziness. This kind of dizziness can occur as outbursts of fooling around or as a momentary desire to shake the order and disturb a fixed way of behaving. In these games also the rough and brutal sides of personality may become visible, e.g., in many rhymes children break taboos, flout authorities and laugh at adults (Abrams 1969; Opie and Opie 1970a).

Matti Bergström (1996) is a brain researcher. The brain stem, the cortex and the limbic system are the parts of the brain that correspond to play acting. The brain stem feeds chaotic impulses to the limbic system whereas the cortex stands for order. Bergström discusses play dominated by impulses from the brain stem (black play) and from the cortex (white play). It is clear that Bergström's black play corresponds to Caillois' *ilinx* whereas 'white' 'educational' play mainly corresponds to competition and imitation. According to Bergström, 'black' play does not last long because the brain does not work for a long time without any kind of order.

Searching for dizziness also occurs in an adult's life in the form of parachute jumps, slalom, rally racing or motor biking. Technical developments have expanded the role of *ilinx* by bringing to amusement parks different kinds of machines that allow people to experience increasing vertigo.

The combinations of the main categories of play

Play does not always belong solely to one of the four main categories. Much play has elements of several main categories, at the same time. According to Caillois, the combination competition–dizziness is impossible because rules and chaos exclude each other. To link imitation with chance is also impossible because no role taking can change chance or bluff destiny.

But dizziness and chance may occur at the same time. There is the element of dizziness in gambling games. Correspondingly, there are elements of play, 'spectacle' in competition. In children's play acting there are often several layers, for example, when children pretend that they are playing chess or when they say that 'when we play football we actually play ice hockey'.

From play to play culture

Children's play culture is an inseparable part of the general culture of any society. It is also a subculture that demands a special kind of cultural competence. This means that children bring to the improvisations of their make-believe play at least two kinds of knowledge: (1) their own interpretations of cultural identity and roles, social events and ways of interaction; and (2) what they know about how to play (Goldman 1998).

The cultural aspect of play means emphasizing collective experiences. Children are seen primarily as members of their society, and secondarily as individuals. Elements of collective consciousness are typical of any subculture. This is true of children's play culture. The cultural aspect does not only mean an inner attitude but the consciousness becomes collective because children are interacting with each other. They share the same language, understand codes and messages, and see the environment full of meanings in the same way (Hannerz et al. 1982).

Children's play culture can be described as a cognitive map, that children adapt totally or partly, more or less correctly and that they then learn to read. But children are also active map-makers who orientate in imperfect and constantly changing circumstances. Culture offers, instead of a ready-made map, principles for navigation and drawing a map. With the help of these instruments children sketch, improvise and constantly change their maps (Frake 1980).

The image of map-makers who orientate in imperfect and changing circumstances is a good description of the current culture of adults as well as children's own play culture, which is characterized by branching paths, getting lost and possibilities for finding new ways.

Play is part of its time and culture as a whole ▪

The following examples illustrate how children's play culture is dependent on its own particular time and culture:

1 In the 1970s, in the make-believe play of Hopi Indians, children hunted rabbits and made pots and plates by hand (Garvey 1977).
2 Reindeer played an important role in the play of Lap children. Children chased a child holding reindeer horns above their head while the others tried to catch them with their lassos (Itkonen 1948).
3 According to adverts, a Käthe Krause doll in Nazi uniform was 'every girl's dream' in the Germany of the 1930s (Retter 1979).
4 A Japanese or American plastic doll was decorated with henna ornaments in order to correspond to the local ideals of a Moroccan bride in the 1970s (Rossie 1996).
5 In the former East Germany, children in the day care centres played with 'defence toys' while war toys were forbidden at the day care centres of Western societies (Retter 1998).

Historic turning points also affect children's play culture

The collapse of the USSR in 1999 was dramatically and quickly reflected in Russian children's play. The strict guidance of role playing at day-care centres was abandoned, and forbidden play themes were freed from control. Western entertainment programmes were shown on television and new toys were sold in the shops. Power Rangers and Barbies displaced the orthodox 'militia play' and restricted home play. The cherished image of innocent Soviet children broke down (Liuobart 1997).

Gradual change also influences play culture

When we look back in time, we are able to see how play culture has gradually changed. Adults tend to look back through rose-coloured glasses. The Danish researcher, Flemming Mouritsen (1996) writes about play as a cherished ideal in what he sees as the golden 1950s. A rich play culture flourished in an environment that was supported by mothers at home, steady families and dynamic local societies. The countryside was near, children were freed from work and there were enough of them to create friendship groups and to play together.

The Nordic idea of flourishing play culture is not just based on an idealized view of play. Scandinavian folklorists, Finnish Leea Virtanen (1970) and Norwegian Åse Enerstvedt (1982), have shown that children's traditional play culture was vivid and rich even after the 1950s. In the Introduction to her book, *Antti, pantti pakana*, Virtanen agrees with Iona and Peter Opie (1970b) that 'an anthropologist or folklorist does not have to travel far from their home door to find an intuitive play culture that has been very little influenced by the reasonable world of adults'.

Today, the same approach would probably lead to very different results. Any researcher of children's play culture would be unlikely to find much if they stood near children's front doors waiting to see play! This is because children are elsewhere nowadays.

Constancy and change in children's play culture

Play changes with time but an historical examination of play will also emphasise constancy. If we look at the well-known painting by Pieter Brueghel from 1560, we can easily identify children who roll a hoop along the ground, play blind man's buff or leapfrog, in spite of cultural changes and hundreds of years difference (Francastel 1995; Kjörup 1983). Some part of play tradition has proved relatively unchanged from one century to another and from one nation to another. For example, some nonsense rhymes are repeated in numerous countries. The forms and meanings of some games have changed over time whereas the main themes have remained the same. Both those who look for similarities and those who look for differences find what they seek. Play is a phenomenon through which culture imprints its image on children and their culture.

Play culture and gender   ■

The play culture of boys and girls is different

The difference between girls' and boys' play has been identified and proved again after again, even in different cultures. This is evident in the research, and also in what we observe in our daily lives. In Chapter 10 this is explored in more detail.

We find that boys' games are wilder than girls' games; boys imitate remote figures, heroes, soldiers and cowboys whereas girls play more peacefully, imitating what is familiar to them such as home and care-connected pursuits. The same differences are repeated time after time quite independent of the cultural context (Gussin-Paley 1984).

Are the differences innate or due to child-rearing practices? It is hard to answer this question. It is a fact that the gender distinction is reflected as a main theme throughout the cultures of the world. We need to build this fact into the way we look at children's play culture. When we study children's own play culture, we need to bear in mind that there will be separate boys' play and girls' play as well as joint play.

Culture *for* children and *of* children   ■

Children's culture consists of two parts. Culture *for* children is produced by adults for children, whereas culture *of* children is created by the children themselves (Danbolt and Enerstvedt 1995).

Culture for children:

- traditionally consists of children's literature, drama and music;
- less traditionally, it consists of media products such as films, television, videos and computer games;
- includes products of high quality that stimulate the development of a child;
- but it also includes commercial junk culture.

Children's own play culture consists of:

- play acting of stories, songs, rhymes, gibberish, riddles;
- jokes, contextual teasing, bantering and making noises;
- adding and adapting ideas they take from the media;
- the creative use of toys and other materials;
- skills that increase the play cultural competence but are only meaningful in play situations.

Knowing a new nonsense rhyme or a joke, or inventing an unexpected episode in the spirit of an admired television programme, might well raise the status of the child in a play group, but this seldom overlaps with the goals that adults have for children (Mouritsen 1996).

Age matters

Play culture changes according to the age of the children. What a research study finds out about the play culture of 10-year-olds cannot be taken as representative of the play culture of 6-year-olds. Although the interest in this book is not to examine the correlation between age, type of play and developmental level, this has to be taken into account.

For example, when we look at the youngest children, we cannot say there is any evidence of children's own play culture as they have not yet developed the essentials that are needed in order to be a full member of a group playing together. These essentials are:

• commonly shared knowledge;
• shared values;
• shared experiences;
• shared ways of thinking;
• the same language (or non-verbal ways of communicating);
• shared ways of understanding codes.

The older children lead the play culture

Those who really construct, maintain and deconstruct children's play culture are often the oldest in a spontaneously gathered play group. Today there are remarkably fewer groups of children playing together with a wide age range. The strict age segregation that exists nowadays in Finnish and other societies is reflected in the children's play culture. In the past, the 6-year-olds were apprentices, but now children's play culture at the day-care centres is led by the 6-year-olds, who are the oldest within these settings. [Editor's note. In England, because children often enter reception classes at four years of age it is usually the 3-year-olds who have to take on this responsibility.] This means that, instead of the traditional way, when children's play culture is transferred from one generation, to the next 'with little jumps' (Hannerz 1982; Mouritsen 1996), the transfer has to happen faster and earlier.

What do we mean by the children's *own* play culture?   ■

In the past, this has often been interpreted as play that has been transferred from one generation of children to the next without any adult intervention. This has directed the attention of the researchers towards children's lore, game starting rhymes, riddles, jokes and clapping games. Together with games with rules this area has formed the core of play culture, the 'true' play culture (Virtanen 1970; Enerstvedt 1982; Ekrem 1990; Opie and Opie 1970). In reality, a 'pure' play culture is an unlikely phenomenon, and is more unlikely the younger the children are. We begin to see how artificial, if not impossible, absolute boundaries are in relation to children's play culture.

As we have seen, childhood today is characterized by:

- institutionalization
- age segregation
- the powerful influence of mass media.

The boundary between culture for children created by adults and the children's own play culture is also obscure. In practice, culture for children (as well as adult culture), forms part of children's common experience, and provides the tools and materials of their play culture.

This potential cultural material becomes the children's through its use and adaptation in their play acting. The process is similar to the one that changes the story of *The Wind in the Willows* into a theatrical production. Also the step from a book or a film to pretend play demands:

- a manuscript;
- casting;
- developing the plot;
- acting and speaking the lines;
- making it their 'own' by both imitating and creating.

In addition, it also demands materials, time to develop the play, and space away from adult intervention.

Children's play culture flourishes in corners where adults do not reach   ■

Making their own space allows children the opportunity to create their own imagined worlds. The boundaries of children's play culture are unclear but like any subculture it filters material for its own purposes from what is offered by the dominant culture. Then this material is strengthened and worked on according to unspoken cultural codes by the children.

Although the worlds of adults and children intertwine and overlap with each other, in many ways the children's own play culture is the area of childhood where they act most on their own and without compulsion or without adults directing them in adult-chosen tasks.

Questions for reflective practice

- Reflect on the view that children don't play in order to learn, although they learn while they are playing.
- Do you see world events reflected in the play of the children you are working with?
- What is the difference between adult-led child culture and children's own play culture?
- Compare children's culture made by adults for children with children's own play culture and state how you see this in your work with children and families.

Further reading

Schwartzman, H. (1978) *Transformations: The Anthropology of Children's Play*. New York: Plenum Press.
Vygotsky, L. (1976) Play and its role in the mental development of the child. In J. Bruner, A. Jolly and K. Sylva (eds) *Play: Its Role in the Development and Evolution*. New York: Basic Books, 537–54. (This is a lecture in Russian in 1933, published in English in 1966.)

4

COMPETITIONS AND GAMES IN CHILDREN'S PLAY CULTURE

Competition – winning and losing

In the world that adults have created for themselves, competitive games form a major part. Competitive games have also been created by adults for young children to participate in. In Finnish day-care centres, children are introduced to many games, where winning and losing are central elements. However, the rules are defined by adults, and the children's contribution to developing the rules is minimal in these games, which are planned, organized and led by adults. Because these types of games have no child-initiated element, they are not included in this book.

Children develop their own competition play, away from adults

However, we do find children developing their own play in ways which involve them in competition. This kind of play (which the French theorist Caillois has called competition (*agon*) play), can be found away from adults.

On a cloudy afternoon two girls play a game that is a form of hide-and-seek with rules called *kirkonrotta* 'church rat' in the playground at the Kesäkumpu day-care centre. Miia is standing with her face to the wall. Tiina is patting Miia's back with her hands in time with what she says:

A newly washed clean rat . . .
Miia: Back!

Tiina chants it again: A newly washed clean back, refreshed with Rexona [soap], who was the one . . . how was it?
Miia: Who touched it last?
Tiina and Miia finish the rhyme together: With his dirty hands, a circle and a cross, who touched it last?
Miia turns around and says: Tiina! (There are no other alternatives.)
Tiina answers: Right! Say the number!
Miia: Fifty!
Tiina: Yes!

Tiina starts to count, facing the wall. Tiina counts to ten. She does this five times and then starts to seek the other children. Miia is found very near. 'Miia-rat seen!'

Antti has 'just learnt' the game. His rhyme is shorter but the rules for the play are very clear to him. The seeker is not allowed to be a 'home rat' but has to seek far from home so that children (rats) who are hiding can come and say 'Own rat saved, all the rats saved.'

Knowing the rules, and obeying them are important parts of competitive play. The game 'church rat' clearly shows the characteristics involved in Callois' competition category of play:

- children develop their own arbitrary rules for the play;
- the children define these rules themselves together;
- they obey the rules they have made;
- they create a space for the play;
- the children assume that each child participating will do their best to win;
- there is agreement that the rules apply to each child equally.

Does it matter who wins and who loses?

We have to ask, are the children really taking part in a competition? No-one seems to bother about who wins and who loses, but an element of competition is there. You have to avoid the role of the chaser by hiding so well that you are not the first to be found. It is better to be found last, and it is best of all to be the one who saves all the others.

Only at the beginning of the game is the role of the seeker left purely to chance. This is because the rhyme said by one of the players defines the role of the seeker. After that a victorious player needs to be quick, ingenious and a good tactician. A slower and less inventive player does not save the others and so becomes the chaser more often than the others.

So, although everybody has the same rules and equal opportunities in theory, personal differences also make a difference in practice. Each child playing can partly choose how they participate. One child might take on the role of 'co-runner', another might seek momentary heroism by saving everybody just before the game is over. After all, there is nothing like the genuine joy of being a hero!

At the same time, children avoid categorizing each other as 'good' or 'poor' players while playing these kinds of games. Children regulate the element of competition skilfully so that the competitive side does not become too dominant. To be good at chess or football is different from being good at 'church rat'.

The most important thing about competitive play is being together in a group

The motive for playing 'church rat' is not simply about competition. It is absolutely not about winning the game. Entering the world of play, a world defined by arbitrary rules and repetition, means coming together, belonging to the group and sharing the excitement of the game. Playing together is the primary motive, competition is secondary. Yet, the game loses its point if the element of competition is entirely removed because then there would be no reason to find a good place to hide oneself or save the others by using courage.

Competitive games the children know

The 6-year-olds often know several games with rules and competition. Sanna explains how to play 'tar pot'. She says: 'There is a pot and we make our own nests round it and there has to be a stick and you throw it behind somebody and you have to start running around the pot and if you get to the nest of the other, the other one has to go running.'

They also play 'mirror and colour'. Sofia says: 'If you have something green you can take five giant's steps and so on.'

'Horse' is Tiia's own version of blind man's buff. At least three players are needed. The horse shuts her eyes and tries to find the others who stand without moving.

Six-year-olds have many versions of tag. Noora describes how they play 'ball straddle tag', 'Moomin tag' and 'kiss tag'. In 'ball straddle tag' when you get caught you have to 'roll like this round your legs and then you are free again'.

The children use ideas from stories in the *Moomin* books by Tove Jansson are of international repute, and have been translated into English. Noora also says,

When you play Moomin tag you crouch down and if you say 'Moomintroll' you are safe. But if you say 'Groge' you become the catcher. You can only say names from *Moomin* books and videos, but you cannot say 'spruce' because it is only a tree not a Moomin. You can say Snufkin, Snork Maiden or Little My . . . but Groge only if you want to become the chaser. It is the only way to become the chaser if you want to be it, or you have to slow down on purpose.

'Moomin tag' is like ordinary tag except that you get safe by means of naming characters from the Moomin books. A traditional tag game tells us, through its rules, something about current children's culture and children's cultural competence. It is easy to add new elements to the rules of a traditional game if they are based on widely known themes like the Moomin books. For example, by throwing a Moomin character's name into the game, the rarer the character, the more fascinating.

Current additions to traditional games of tag enable endless variations. 'President tag' is an example of a short-lived version. You save yourself by saying the name of a candidate for president of Finland but you are not allowed to repeat the previous name and the name of one of the candidates, Esko Aho, who is like 'Groge' in 'Moomin tag'. If you say that, you become chaser. It is easy to guess that this version of tag was of interest before the presidential election in Finland.

The basic rule of kiss tag is simple. When a girl chases and catches a boy, she is allowed to kiss him. If a game is to be seen as successful by the children, then every player must be involved and has to agree with the rules. This is not always the case in kiss tag. It is typical for this game to start without a shared agreement. Girls just start to run after boys – or the reverse. Girls, boys and kissing create a tension in this game and the enjoyment of this game is to maintain this tension.

The element of competition can be traced in all of these examples:

- In 'church rat' the one who is found last or the one who rescues the others is the best.
- In 'mirror and colour', the one who first touches the back of the leader is the best.
- In tag play the 'winner' is the one who does not get chased.

Elements in play

There are glimpses of dizzy play during competitive play that is going well. The temptation to develop a carnival spirit, with high jinx which turn the world upside down, which Callois calls 'dizzy' or *ilinx* play can often be glimpsed in children's competitive play. For example, someone stops to do his or her best for a moment and slows down on purpose in order to get chased. However, too much of this destroys the game.

There are also moments of imitation and make-believe in competition play. It is also possible to combine elements of competition in play with the kind of imitation and make-believe which we shall look at later in the book, described by Callois as 'mimicry'.

Juuso describes how the boys play 'ice-hockey-football'.

> I am the leader of football because we pretend that it is ice-hockey. I am Timo Jutila. He is the captain of the league. Mika is Ville Peltonen and then I am, or Mika is Timo Jutila, I am Saku Koivu and Jarmo Myllys, Jukka is Jukka Tammi and then Jonas is Mika Strömberg.

Finland won the World Championship in 1995 and the players became idols, even for small boys. This shows in many ways in their play acting. The competition found in games played by adults, such as ice-hockey, even reaches small boys.

When ice-hockey is combined with football in the way the boys have done, something qualitatively new is created. In 'ice-hockey-football' boys compete and imitate competition at the same time. When Juuso plays football as Timo Jutila, the element of imitation and pretending changes the nature of competition. The glory of victory and the responsibility for defeat can be shared with the role figure. Taking the role means the winners experience the flush of the World Championship. It makes them heroes too.

A goal is welcomed with triumph. The individual player receives honour, but so does his league. In other games, hiding cunningly, flying quickly and saving the others dramatically creates an essential part of the fascination of playing.

In their own competitive play, children are in control, not adults ∎

In the games we explore in this chapter, children create a situation that is under their control, without explaining anything to anybody. They can use their strength without worrying about whether they are popular. They can play with children they usually shun or are afraid of. Every child can confidently give orders when it is their turn, tease, throw a ball at another child, pretend to be dead or kiss the one being chased. When involved in this kind of competitive play, children can confidently do things that would, in other situations, mean they would be driven out of the play by the other children.

In their own games with rules, children regulate the impact of competition skilfully, so that it does not become too dominant:

- by not having qualifying races, or selecting players;
- by avoiding categories of 'good' and 'poor' players while playing these kinds of game;
- by creating 'handicaps' which equalize so that one player is not superior compared to others (which would threaten the game by making it too predictable, boring or dull).

The present, past and future of competitive (*agon*) play

Games like 'church rat' played by Miia and Tiina, are examples of children's own play culture which moves from one generation of children to the next without adult intervention. But there are only two players, so we only get a glimpse of the game, because it doesn't really belong in the context of the day-care centre. It originates in the backyard at home, where it would traditionally be played by a mixed group of boys and girls of different ages.

It is significant that Miia, who knows 'church rat' so well that she can teach it to Tiina with the traditional rhyme and rules, has got a backyard at home.

Miia and Antti are the only children who know the game well, both the rhyme and the rules. Emilia has played it, but without the rhyme. Anu, Jonas, Joni, Petri and Mikael have also played this game a few times. Again, all of them have a backyard where they live, and a group of boys and girls of different ages to play with. Restriction on space, asphalt and litter do not make a backyard unfit for play, but lack of a group of children to play with does.

Noora, Jenna, Jukka, Katariina, Maija, Maria and Tomi have not even heard about 'church rat'. Tuomas says uncertainly 'Maybe I have heard about this game, if it is like swivelling the skipping rope on the ground while others jump.' In fact, 'church rat' and 'mouse tail' are two different games. Emmi doesn't know the game. In addition, she shows her lack of experience of playing in the backyard with other children at home by stating: 'I only have friends to play with here (at the day-care centre) because no one knows where I live.'

For these children, the playground at the day-care centre is the only place where they can learn and play competitive games of their own making. Despite offering enough space, time and friends to play with, the institutional playground does not compensate for the lack of playing in the backyard at home.

Mixed ages matter if children are to develop sophisticated competition play

Play needs competent players. At the day-care centre 6-year-olds are the oldest and most competent players. They are also, according to the theory practised by Marita, the kindergarten teacher, 'at the age of games with rules'. This means that 6-year-olds are ready to play these kinds of games, but the problem is where they can learn them.

The age segregation at the day-care centre breaks the smooth transfer of competitive play from the older to the younger children. For example, only two children out of 23 knew 'church rat' so well that they could have taught it to others.

Large groups of children constrain the play

Another problem at the day-care centres is the number of children. There are too many children. In the backyard at home, 'church rat' play can take up the whole space, but in the playground at the day-care centre this kind of game must be played in among other players, the majority of whom have not yet reached 'the age of games with rules'. These younger children are neither interested in nor yet capable of playing 'church rat'.

Are the games with rules that children make still vital?

It is also worth asking whether these kinds of game still appeal to children. Does the example of Tiina learning the game from Miia prove that these games are still vital? Is it the case that in spite of all the changes in society, children still do manage to transfer their own play culture from one generation of children to the next, as they have always done?

Play in which children make their own rules and competitions, especially traditional street play, has notably declined. In the 1950s it was typical to children to play in their backyards. Now there are seldom groups of children playing in the backyards. Children are elsewhere.

Where are the children now when they are not to be found playing in the backyard?

Television and an increase in hobbies introduced at an early age compete for the children's attention. In addition, age segregation and, in Finland, decreasing birth rates have led to the fact that there are not enough children playing in the backyard during the best hours for play.

Eva-Lis Bjurman (1981) states that children, especially socially advantaged children, spend a great deal of time on hobbies, which are believed to train individual performance. Emmi demonstrates this phenomenon. She has three hobbies a week. She visits theatre and art exhibitions with her mother, and she only plays with other children at the day-care centre.

The play culture of more disadvantaged children is threatened by moving from one place to another, the restrictions experienced by the adults, a poor environment, mass culture, and poorly planned housing in less popular suburbs.

Stephen Kline (1995) suggests that television steals time from play as well as from reading books or common family meals. The fragmented pattern of the day contrasts with the regular scene of the 1950s when, after supper, all the children went to the backyard to play together. If you wanted to do this nowadays, you may well find yourself alone in the backyard.

Changes in play

The direction of change in play is clear. There are fewer and fewer games of this type and they are played less often. Between 1950 and 1970, Finnish, Norwegian and British folklorists collected huge quantities of materials of children's own play culture. For example, Iona and Peter Opie in the UK (1970a, 1970b, 1993) mention around two hundred traditional games and rhymes. In this book, the 6-year-old children, the oldest in the day-care centres, only knew a few traditional games and rhymes. Although we can suppose that the children have not yet acquired full competence in this kind of play, it is still clear that play with rules and competitions of the children's own making has notably declined. What does this change mean?

How do children's games with rules and competition compare with those devised by adults?

It is fruitful to compare children's games with adult-directed games because of the common element of competition. Perhaps moving from 'church rat' through ice-hockey-football to ordinary football does not seem a very dramatic thing to do, but the difference in quality of the competition is fundamental. The element of competition takes on a different meaning when adults define the rules of the game. There is a shift from a 'culture *of* children' to adult-created 'culture *for* children'.

A trophy in the glass cabinet at the day-care centre demonstrates the change. The newspaper *Helsingin Sanomat* (1997) writes about the big football tournament between kindergartens: 'The attitude of the referee was rather loose. Any kind of throw-in was accepted, despite the fact that most of the six-year-olds can throw correctly from behind the neck.' In a real game of football, it is adult-created rules that are followed. Winners and losers are named publicly. 'To be good at football' is a relatively consistent label for some children. In games from the play culture of children, such as 'church rat' A and B teams are not needed.

One can, of course, argue that 6-year-olds' football is a form of play, as is 'church rat' and 'ice-hockey-football' in spite of emphasizing competition and the adult-centred rules of the game. The newspaper announces: 'The day-care centre football trophy was once again the joy of the children.' However, we can see that the change in the quality of competition is fundamental. Paradoxically, competition becomes more visible in situations where adults try to fade it out.

The competitive element in adult-created games cannot be hidden or disguised

Marianne Liliequist (1993) describes a Swedish city block football match for 7-year-olds. She says that the adults are anxious to soften and disguise the competitive aspects, wanting instead to promote democracy. However, this approach is certain to fail, because the game follows its own logic. The reality is that it highlights the children whose motor skills are weak. Children shout at the girls who are afraid of the ball, and at the boys who blunder.

It is not possible to play football in the same spirit as 'church rat' because the primary starting point of football is unequivocable. It is about competition. The very idea of the game is watered down if it is run in the spirit of 'total equality'. If this is done, then no one is satisfied with the game. This is because the game of football depends on the fact that all the players are on a sufficiently equal level to create and maintain the tension that motivates everybody to do their best. This is why there are A and B leagues for adults, and we now find these imitated in the A and B teams of the day-care centres.

However, the inevitable discrimination that is embedded in A and B categorization is more marked at the day-care centre than in the junior teams of the sports clubs. Children do not come to the day-care centre because they are enthusiastic about football or becoming a good player. Consequently the leagues are formed by choosing the best players among an ordinary age class. The result is that there are fewer girls than boys in the leagues. The staff of the Hilapieli day-care centre explain to parents who suspect a sexist attitude that it is necessary to drop girls from the football team who 'admire clouds' or 'kick pebbles' and do not concentrate on the required exercises.

For many girls it probably does not make any difference if they belong to the league or not, whereas for many boys, it is a painful experience to be rejected from the league because doing well in sports and other physical trials is a measure of acceptance for them. This is why belonging to the league may have an impact on a child's position in the peer group. According to Judith Rich Harris (1998), the comparisons inside the peer group often have long-lasting effects on a child's sense of self-identity in ways which give children lasting labels as successes or as failures.

Children naturally compare themselves with others

In the book *Birdy* by William Wharton, the characters Birdy and Al state, 'Competition is something we have invented in order to help us forget that we have forgotten how to play. To play is something that is done for its own sake.' This does not mean that children would not themselves organize running races and other games where the winners and losers are defined as unambiguously as in ice hockey or football matches led by adult trainers. The starting point of the theory of social comparison takes as granted that human beings have a tendency to compare themselves with others. This is why situations where this is possible are also attractive. The key issue is whether a child competes voluntarily or is led by an adult.

Although children's own competitive *agon*-play is carried out according to their needs, this does not eliminate conflicts in the game, leading to situations or problems linked to the position of children of different ages. Rather, playing together is an optimal way of solving problems that emerge out of group play together. In children's naturally formed groups, they do not try to decrease the friction by forming as homogenous groups as possible according to age, sex or skills. Instead children try to find 'the lowest common denominator' on which the game can be constructed. The tolerance in these games with rules is high compared to adult-directed team games.

Culture for children, organized by adults

The proportion of children's own competitive play is decreasing, and the proportion of adult-directed games, especially team games, is increasing. This means a shift towards hardening competition. Football tournaments between kindergartens did not exist in the 1950s and children under school age (which is 7 years old in Finland) did not participate in training at sports clubs. In contrast, ice-hockey has been a hobby for 'many years' for some 6-year-olds of today, for example, Mika calls it his 'advanced hobby'.

Mika plays ice-hockey with enthusiasm but Jukka's attitude towards boys' games is ambivalent:

Jukka: I am no longer in a football team or ice hockey team, I don't want to, I'm going to basketball, probably basketball . . .
MK: You now want to play basketball?
Jukka: Yes, if I get there. Daddy says that I should first skate well, so I can get to Jokerit ice hockey team. Recently I was in HIFK. When I can skate well, I'll go to Jokerit, there they play real matches.
. . .
MK: Do you play football?
Jukka: In HJK I have trained and our league always lost the game, except once, with the 'whites'. Then the match ended in a draw.
MK: You finished that?
Jukka: I didn't say to the trainer that I don't play any more.
MK: You just thought to stop playing?
Jukka: I just decided.
MK: You don't like it any longer?
Jukka: No, because we always go to the sand field and there you can fall in sand.
MK: You don't like it because you can hurt yourself?
Jukka: Yes, you can hurt yourself. When somebody trips you up you can fall straight to sand. And then your knee might bleed, it's no fun, and it can come to your stomach, too . . . one boy from our league, Make, hurt himself and his knee was bleeding and when I went to play I avoided Make because he had wounds.

Jukka's talk reflects the contradiction between ideals and reality. The idol of this little boy is a skilful skater who plays real matches in Jokerit. In reality, Jukka is afraid of participating in the hard game and harsh measures which are part of playing football. Consequently, he moves from one sport and league to another trying to find his place on the fields where games are played according to adult-directed rules. He wants to fulfil the wishes of his father but it is far from easy.

Towards greater gender separation

With the decline of children's own competitive play, the commonly shared area of boys' and girls' play culture is decreasing. In street games girls and boys have equal opportunities, whereas team games strengthen gender segregation. Although team games are not forbidden for girls, girls seldom choose this kind of hobby. Girls who do enjoy them are not discriminated against, but the same pattern seems to repeat itself time after time. Girls are simply not as interested as boys in ice hockey or football.

Of course, there are many activities other than team games that compensate for the disappearance of street play, but whatever they are, it seems that the final result is that boys will be boys, and girls will be girls, increasingly separated into their own groups. Hobbies are chosen according to gender at an early age, and so are television programmes.

The future of children's competitive play

Traditional games in a new context

There does seem to be a desire among 6-year-olds to learn traditional games. These games seem to represent an important layer of competition/*agon* play, with its child-made rules and competitive elements. Indeed, Ulrich Beck, Anthony Giddens and Christopher Lash (1994) emphasize that a post-traditional society does not mean a society without traditions but a society where traditions are given new meanings and where they are applied in a new context.

Traditional games are not about symbols or nostalgia for children

Children are not aware of traditions in the same way as adults, who often use them to create atmosphere, or to be nostalgic. Traditional games are played by children for their own sake. This is why it is interesting to find that traditional competitive *agon* games still belong to the repertoire of many 6-year-olds. The spontaneous and genuine interest of the child is the factor that persistently maintains the tradition of this kind of play.

Conclusion

We can conclude that the element of competition, its self-regulation, and the self-made and shared rules, all unite and create a feeling of togetherness. Children enjoy being together in a group that appeals to them, and at the same time meets their developmental needs. These social games seem to speak to children in the same way as they have always done, but the circumstances have become less favourable to this kind of play.

The daily schedules of day-care centres and schools set limits on long-lasting games. Children divide into those who have hobbies and those who do not. Competition that is damped down and hidden in children's competitive play appears when 'trainers' come into the picture. Age segregation also changes the transfer of play culture to younger children. If there are no older children who know the games, then the church rat becomes thinner and thinner without the support of adults.

Questions for reflective practice

- Have you considered the value of introducing young children to the formal rules of games such as football?
- Have you observed whether children make their own rules in competitive play in the way suggested in this chapter?
- How does age segregation impact on the play culture of children?
- How much time do children have to develop competition as they use it in their play culture?

Further reading

Opie, I. (1993) *The People in the Playground*. Oxford: Oxford University Press.

Opie, I. and Opie, P. (1970) *Children's Games in Street and Playground*. Oxford: Oxford University Press.

Sutton-Smith, B. (1976) *The Dialectics of Play*. Schorndorf: Verlag Hoffman.

5

GAMES OF CHANCE AND LUCK IN CHILDREN'S PLAY CULTURE: *ALEA*

Is there a place for chance in the play culture of children? By the age of 6, children have become acquainted with the principle of luck and chance in many ways. The National Lottery fascinates Oskari: 'Do you know that a million marks is six circles and one?' Children know about the throw of the die in games like snakes and ladders. Instead of skills it is chance that decides who wins. Caillois calls games where the element of chance is essential *alea*.

Starting rhymes

In this chapter, we shall concentrate on the element of luck only as we find it in rhymes. Leea Virtanen (1970) calls these rhymes 'game starting rhymes', in which typically children will use a well-known rhyme to select the chaser or seeker. Children stand in a circle and the child who is reciting the rhyme points by turns at each of the players. The others wait to see at whom the finger will stop. 'The finger of destiny' decides the roles of the players.

Counting people out of the game

It is easy to name two very well-known rhymes. Even an English speaker can feel the rhythm and rhyme in the words:

Entten tentten
teelikamentten

In such nonsense rhymes children can develop different versions without losing the essence of the rhyme. 'Maalari maalasi taloa' is the other rhyme that is known by most of the 6-year-olds we met. In this rhyme the painter paints the house blue and red, and the departure of the painter is always on the count of, 'puh, pah, pelistä pois', corresponding to the English 'one, two, out you go'. The last words are always the same and are never varied by the players, so that all the children know where they are in the play. The last words demonstrate a cross-cultural feature of children's games, with the typical counting out of the person. This kind of ending seems to emphasize the fact that somebody is hit by good or bad luck.

'Auto ajoi kilparataa' is a rhyme about the car that drove on a racing circuit and lost a tyre. This rhyme is also popular with children, and Niina chants this, using a longer version which has a happy ending when a new tyre leads the car to victory. Henna, Riikka, Tuulia, Miia, Mika, Niina, Jukka, Antti, Tuomas, Sanna, all know these three rhymes, and play them together in the outside play area of the day-care centres they attend.

Using traditional rhymes as a structure to make up your own

Mika makes up a fourth rhyme:

Who won the World Championship, Finland or Sweden, we are going to see it soon, one, two, out you go! I made it up myself!

Once children know the structure and function of traditional nonsense rhymes, they can then replace these with their own 'homemade' rhymes.

Mika, who knows at least three traditional rhymes, can make up his rhyme using the traditional structures. The rhyme reflects:

- a particular event (the World Ice Hockey Championship);
- a personal interest;
- cultural competence (knowing about traditional rhymes of the culture).

Rituals, repetition and phonological awareness

The function of using rhymes is not simply pragmatic. The rituals and repetition in these rhymes increase the fascination of games of chance and luck. When children chant the rhymes, they also have fun twisting the meanings of the words and enjoying alliterations and end rhymes. They can also introduce additions from current advertising, which might be incorporated into the play permanently. For example, we saw earlier that in 'church rat' a well advertised soap product called Rexona is rubbed on the players' backs during the game!

Why is it a good idea to leave things to chance during play in groups?

There are several important reasons for the children leaving things to chance during play in a group setting.

Quarrel-prevention-rhymes

Once children understand the idea of leaving things to chance, they can use rhymes in a number of different situations. Sofia explains 'They are used in all quarrel issues.' She understands the central idea of *chance*. It is possible to avoid conflict if everybody withdraws from using power and leaves the decision in the hands of the impartial laws of chance.

There are a lot of 'quarrel issues' and there are many ways to use 'quarrel prevention rhymes'. Riikka explains that in one game, 'Somebody swivels round the lamp-post and the others sit and when they have swivelled enough they chant and the one who goes out is the one who swivels next.'

Casting roles for the play, using games of chance

In make-believe play, rhymes are often used at the beginning of the play to help in casting the various roles. Because the roles are unequal, this phase is open to many conflicts. Jaana says, 'When we all want to be something like rabbits or mice, we can chant who is the rabbit.' The most wanted role might be a human mother, the mother of a horse, sweeper or the red (in Power Rangers). In all these situations children like Sofia, Emilia, Tuomas and Tiia can turn to chanting.

Rhymes can also be used when something needs to be left somewhere and guarded. Niina says, 'Well, someone has to guard something. If we collect leaves or something, someone has to guard the pile of leaves while the others collect more.'

Using games of chance to share toys

Sharing toys can be a risky business for children. Sanna says, 'I lent an expensive toy to one of my friends but there was someone else in the play, too, and she wanted to have it too, and I tried to give to her as well. I chanted which of them would get it.' Sanna, whether she makes the decision who will play with her toy, or whether she turns to a game of chance to make the decision, is nevertheless using her power as the owner of the toy.

The use of power in games of chance

When a child chooses a play pal by chanting, it is not simply about the harmless allotment of parts. Although Miia finds this way of problem solving 'rather good', Riikka thinks it is cruel:

> If someone plays with somebody and doesn't want to play with someone else, then they can chant, so that the one who goes out is the one they don't want to play with, and then you feel so bad.

The use of power in play is sometimes cruel and can leave a child outside the play, feeling excluded. It is experienced as discrimination and it does not feel any better for the child experiencing it simply because the rejection happens 'by chance'. Cheating is relatively easy:

- Even young children quickly work out who needs the first turn in order to be able to say 'out you go' to another child.
- Children can also quicken or slow down the rhythm so as to get the hoped-for result.
- It is also possible to find a pretext and repeat the rhyme if it goes wrong the first time.

If children want to exclude somebody from play by chance, they can easily do so, and the one who is rejected cannot appeal to fair play if they suspect cheating has been the reason for expelling them from the game.

Many ways of using rhymes

Some of the examples given here are very close to the most traditional use of rhymes in games with rules.

- Children count who has to guard the pile of leaves instead of counting who will be the chaser or seeker.
- When children swivel around the lamp-post, they take turns and it is satisfying to leave the turns to chance, because the turns circulate evenly enough across the children.

In these situations children find that using rhymes makes things:

- as fair as possible
- agreed by everyone.

In make-believe play the role of rabbit, sweeper, mother, the mother of the horse or 'Red' lasts throughout the play and this is one of the reasons why the casting of parts is far from always solved by *chance*. Negotiations are sometimes very prolonged and can, in the worst case, result in the children abandoning the game.

All in all we can say that when children understand the element of chance of rhymes, they can use them for many purposes. By using rhymes children want to guarantee equal opportunities for everybody and create fair play situations. Traditionally rhymes are used in game-starting situations because equality is the central principle of this kind of play acting. Here the rhymes also soften the element of competition because they bring in sequences that are based on chance instead of skills. If the element of chance is connected with the starting points of fantasy play this has to be agreed on separately. If everybody agrees, it is OK to leave the casting to chance. But in more demanding make-believe play there might be only one child who is able to manage the leading role.

Where do you learn rhymes?

Children usually say that they have 'just learned' games and rhymes. Niina, Noora, Miia, Antti and Jonas all say that they have learned rhymes in the backyard. However, the handing on of games is not entirely in the hands of children. Mothers, fathers, grandmothers or grandfathers may have taught their offspring a rhyme they learned as a child. At the day-care centres the children attend, the adults who teach these kinds of rhymes are mostly:

- temporary supply staff;
- conscientious objectors, opting to do community service rather than undertake National Service in the Finnish Army;
- trainees;

- occasionally staff who turn to these rhymes when a conflict threatens: Miika explains that a nursery nurse counts who is allowed to sit on the bean bag during story time.

Kindergarten teachers in Finland seldom teach traditional rhymes, although rhymes are in daily use in most of the day-care centres. Children's own play culture and day-care culture are two different subcultures.

A child who has learned a rhyme from children's television might only partly remember it. When this happens, only the 'plot' of the rhyme stays in the child's mind. Sanna says, 'Yes, a car, it began like a car drove in the motor racing circuit and ended so that the tyre came loose.'

Even children who do not know a single rhyme by heart, still know about rhymes. Only one child, Jukka, argued that he has not heard a single rhyme of this sort. The others identified at least one rhyme that they had heard of.

As we would expect, children who play traditional games regularly are the ones who know more rhymes. Chanting rhymes regularly is naturally the best way to keep the rhymes in mind.

Expert rhyme players are in decline

The decline of these rhymes is parallel to the decline of traditional games with rules that we read about in the last chapter. Fewer rhymes are used, less and less often. It goes without saying that the less children play traditional games, the less children will use rhymes in 'game starting' situations.

How many rhymes can children recite and use as they play?

A child who knows a large number of rhymes is often the one who chants, especially if none of the other players know the rhymes that are used in 'game-starting' situations. Antti says, 'Well, it is always me because the others don't know the rhymes.' Antti can chant another of the rhymes which we looked at earlier in this chapter, 'maalari maalaa'. He can recite this fluently and so can genuinely use it as a game-starting rhyme. On the one hand, he states that he only partly knows the rhyme 'entten, tentten', which we looked at earlier in the chapter. It seems that in the street play of today, knowing a little is enough.

Knowing one rhyme is nothing compared with the play of the

children in the 1950s, who were expert players, and who shone by changing to a different rhyme for every round. When there were quite a few players in the group, and the last one who went out became the chaser, the 'chanter' could show off his or her skills to the other children. When the child who was 'counter' used a new rhyme, it aroused admiration among the other children (Virtanen 1970).

Virtanen found regional variation in the average number of rhymes children mastered from four to eight rhymes. Although these children were aged between 8 to 10 years and without doubt more skilful than 6-year-olds, the decline of knowing rhymes by heart is evident. Today many children become 10-year-olds without 'our backyard' and never add to their rhyme repertoire through active street play during their childhood.

Does it matter if children today don't know rhymes off by heart?

We need to reflect, is there any point in knowing rhymes off by heart? In Finland we have looked down on learning things by heart, including rhymes, for a long time. To know something by heart is considered to be the most primitive kind of learning. Instead we emphasize the importance of 'learning how to learn' and knowing how to search for information. In school, children do not learn songs and rhymes by heart in the way they used to do. Although the cultural competence that children require of each other in their own play culture does not necessarily echo what the school requires for learning, it is possible that the lack of experience they have of learning by heart is indirectly reflected in play.

Questions for reflective practice ▮

- Observe the games with rules that children develop for themselves. Do these resonate with those developed by the children in this chapter?
- How serious is the decline of games with rhymes for children in the first six years?
- How does this link with the importance of the development of phonological awareness as children learn to read and write?
- If adults teach children rhymes, is that enough, or should there also be emphasis on creating environments in which children are able to develop their own games with rhymes and rules?

Further reading ∎

Opie, I. and Opie, P. (1970) *The Lore and Language of School Children.* Oxford: Oxford University Press.

Opie, I. and Opie, P. (1985) *The Singing Game.* Oxford: Oxford University Press.

Ouvry, M. (2004) *Sounds Like Play,* London: Early Education.

Piaget, J. (1952) *Play, Dreams and Imitation.* Trans. C. Gattegno and F. Hodgson. London: Routledge and Kegan Paul.

6

THE WORLD OF MAKE-BELIEVE 1:
FAMILY PLAY SCENARIOS

When children are involved in play that imitates real life, or indulge in fantasy, pretend and role play, they play 'as if' the play scenario is real, rather than 'for real'. Players pretend they believe, or they make themselves or the other children believe, that they are somebody else. Caillois calls this kind of make-believe play *mimicry*.

Sharing an illusion is part of play

When children play together, they share an illusion. To do this, players must make sure that the ideas of each player correspond well enough with others taking part in the play. This happens through communicating with the other children on three levels (Cook-Gumperz 1986):

- *Narrative speech or third-person speaker identity*. The child who becomes the storyteller constructs the plot and episodes, describes, organizes and comments on the other children's play acting. 'No, Kroko should come here first and say, "You will soon become . . .".'
- *In-character-speech*. A child talks in role according to their character, 'You will soon become steak!'
- *Real-life talk*. The talk relates to the reality outside the play, which is still connected to the inner reality of play. Tuomas says, 'Don't drop these or you can't play! Who dropped them?'

When the inner reality of play is genuinely shared, play gets carried away. When players put their soul into the inner world of play, it is possible to become deeply involved. The experience of flow is strong (Bruce 1991).

The importance of imitation in make-believe play

Imitation is central to make-believe play. Even though players might be pretending, and create a world of make-believe, the real world is still imitated in detail. The world of fantasy is hugely about imitating. Children in their fantasy play:

- use as their starting point the real world;
- add in their own fantasy ideas;
- add in other elements, such as stories from books;
- use what they learn from adults and other children;
- make creative combinations of the real world, together with their fantasies and the world of fiction in stories.

In this chapter we shall examine themes that are of current interest for the 6-year-old children we met in previous chapters. We shall look at playing families, the relationship between man and woman, adventures and fights.

Make-believe play using family themes

Playing houses is traditionally seen as play where family members are involved, but dolls can also be in the roles of human children. This is the way children themselves define playing houses.

However, not all girls nowadays feel comfortable playing with dolls. Girls who have a reserved attitude towards traditional play with dolls may find ways of using family life themes by playing, for example, with turtles. Changing human figures into turtles does not cause significant changes in the course of the play, but it does make creative details possible. For example, in the play now discussed, the 'little ones' (the baby turtles) hit on the idea that the shell of Mum-turtle can serve as a playground slide.

Otherwise the uninterrupted dialogue that lasts for one and a half hours is 'family life' rather than a 'turtle-bound' theme. The girls could, for most of the play, use dolls just as effectively as the plastic turtles they have selected. Even the 'turtle-bound' lines are about family life if we look at their central meaning. The episode with the playground slide tells us a great deal about the relationship between mother and child just as distinctly as other episodes.

The framework of the play is as follows:

- There are five turtles. The two biggest turtles are mothers, the two small ones are children and the medium-sized turtle is the big brother (Figure 6.1).

- Riikka has the roles of 'little ones' and moves the smallest turtles around.
- Iida talks for the mothers.
- Big brother occurs in the play only once in a while, and the girls take turns in moving this turtle.
- The girls stay for about an hour at the table in the home area and then go in search of adventure at sea, which is on the floor of the home area and in the hall of the day-care centre.

The 'little ones' have fun. They run and swim, swing and climb, escape and return home, play and eat. Mothers take care of everything. They prepare meals and put the children to bed when it is time, they calm down the little ones when they get too wild and offer help when needed.

Mum: First we shall have our morning meal. You have to eat it.
Child: Why?
Mum: Let me see, tea for morning meal . . .
Child: Yum-yum.
Mum: And you know what else . . . sandwiches with ham!

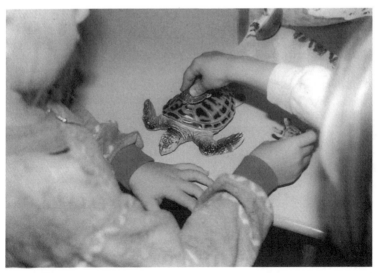

Figure 6.1 Riikka and Miia play with turtles. When Mum takes her 'little one' on her back they are ready to go home.

Child delighted: Yum-yum!
Mum: And milk too!
Child: Yum-yum!
Mum: And then I have a little surprise for you. Ice-cream for dessert!
Child sighing with satisfaction: Ooh!

Nurturing belongs to the basic duties of a mother

A good mother knows what is good for the child (milk and ham sandwiches) and what makes the child happy (ice-cream surprise). Mother gives and the child thankfully receives.

Little turtles go to each other's houses to play

They negotiate with their mothers about how long they are allowed to stay. They get extra time but finally it is time to return home. Mother Anna who has come to pick up her child stands in the doorway and the other mother Suvi suggests: 'Can she stay here overnight I could take care of them.'

Anna: No, she has to come home now.
The child interrupts.   I don't want to!
Anna: You come home now, one hour [the extra time] is already gone, all right?
Child whines: It hurts, I can't walk!
Anna conciliating: Well, climb on my back . . . I can help you . . . here we go . . .
Child: Thank you for your help, Mum!
Anna: Bye, bye and thank you!
Child: Bye, bye!
Suvi: Bye, bye!

Mothers protect children's play

In another part of the play, the big brother is sent after his little sister. The mother in charge takes a peep in the nursery, comes back and says. 'No, they are involved in their play, we cannot disturb them.' The big brother has to wait until the 'good play' is over before he can return home with his little sister.

Parents and children negotiate

These examples not only reflect the children's custom of visiting each other in order to play together, but they also show how Finnish parents and children negotiate. The 'wants' of children are considered as far as possible within the boundaries of other 'musts'. In the first sequence, the extra time, asked on the telephone, is permitted and 'the small ones' can continue playing for one more hour. 'She has to come home now' and 'you come home now' define the boundary where 'the must' of going to sleep exceeds 'the want' of the players. Mother Anna is firm but does not lose her temper. Nor does she begin evaluating whether 'the hurting' is real or not, but simply takes the child on her back (which is definitely easier for a turtle mother than a human mother) and goes home. The latter sequence reflects adults' values towards play. 'Good play' is of such a high value that big brother has to wait.

Mothers have to deal with problems as children play together

Mothers have to tackle all kinds of questions during the day.

Child complaining: Mum, big brother teased me!
Big brother: Why, it was only joking!
Mum: Yes, but you must not tease the younger ones, not even as a joke!

This mother knows what is permitted and forbidden, what is right and wrong. She corrects and comforts when needed:

Mum: Oh, the two of you, you are too wild! Did you break your nail?
Child: Yes.
Mum: Oh, let me see . . . I will cut it . . . come here.

Lost children and loving reunions

The events proceed without interruption. The life of 'the little ones' is free from care and the tasks of the mothers are endless. Suddenly, the mothers notice that their children have run away. When the mothers find the runaways, one of them loudly shouts: 'Mum!'

Mum exclaims: There you are, I have been longing for you so much!
Child: Mum!
Mum: Why did you run away, why!

'Why did you run away?' is an outburst from a mother who knows the pain caused by a lost child. The relief of finding the child overrides the desire to correct the child. Once again, the turtle child is taken on the mother's turtle back and taken home.

The warm and close relationship between mother and child is repeatedly described in the dialogue:

Child: Now I have to go home. (Opens the door.) It is wonderful to come home. I love you Mum! You are the best Mum in the whole world, no one can be a better Mum than you are!
Mum answers in the same tone: Come here to Mum's lap, I will cuddle you. 'Oh, my dear child, I love you so, come here to my lap.'

Home is a warm nest but the tension between home and the outside world still exists. The running away forebodes longer trips away from home and back again. In the last sequence of the play 'the little ones' follow a 'lonely boy' to the sea but return after a long journey.

Different kinds of communication between the players – the dominance of talking in role

It is striking how rarely the girls use talk that organizes the playing. The speech is almost entirely 'in role'. There seems to be an inner understanding between the girls as the play scenario unfolds. This is certainly due to the fact that the girls are able to master the theme of the play exceptionally well. There is also an unspoken understanding about the relationship between mother and child. Love and care form the basis of the relationship. However, it is evident that it is not only their personal experiences that are used as material in their play. The cultural competence of these 6-year-olds makes it possible for them to mix idealized stereotypes in the relationship between mother and child, with their own experiences.

This becomes even clearer when the play with turtles is compared with Riikka's playacting houses. In the public scene of the day-care centre Riikka avoids the most intimate and personal material. For example, when playing houses her parents' divorce is presented in her play. Riikka plays with small cars. She takes the black one, places it far away from the others and explains: 'This is Dad. He doesn't like Mum or children.' An orange car is Mum around whom all the other cars (children) gather.

Experimenting with growing up and leaving home

The external events of the play faithfully imitate real life. At the same time, in this make-believe play, 'emotional speech' is as important as the lines that describe what happens. The play with turtles is a narrative on various different levels that the girls tell about themselves to themselves. Mia and Riikka tell the story about their own growth. The trips the turtles make form wider and wider circles around the home nest.

At the beginning of the story 'the little ones' run on the beach, then they run away. Finally, they sail out onto the open sea. The expanding circles of play and life reach from the table to the hall of the day-care centre.

If, gradually, children are supposed to expand their territory without fear and anxiety, they have to be able to trust in the predictable nature and unquestioning acceptance of the 'mother'. The drive to explore and the need for care occur alternately and need to be satisfied equally. It is significant that Mum takes the runaway in her arms.

Full-time working mothers, big sisters and babies

In their play, other girls tell us about full-time working mothers, who take their children to McDonald's, and about big sisters who go shopping. There are wild and timid babies according to the mood of the players. Although the theme is the same, the variation is rich, which proves how sharp the girls' observations are in the field of human relationships.

Big sisters

The role of the big sister is of special interest. Sometimes the big sister acts like a second mother, sometimes she is expressly what the mother is not. Anu says, 'Well, big girls go shopping and they are allowed to do what they want. They go shopping and buy whatever they want and then they just go somewhere far away, in some parks or . . .'

In the life of a big sister there is much more freedom and fewer responsibilities than in the life of the mother. Big girls do what they want to do. This is why their life is qualitatively different from the life of mothers and little children. The life of big girls is partly elsewhere. This is why imitating them does not show the abundance of detail that is typical in the play about family life at home. Mothers live lives full of 'musts', while big girls have more space for their 'wants'.

At the same time the big sister can tell the same story as little turtles heading out for adventures at sea, as we saw in the story of gradually breaking away from home and growing independent. The direction of life for big sisters is – at least in some cases – away from home whereas mother looks after the home. Even when a mother does shift working, and has to leave her baby with her own sister, the baby is still in her mind.

Babies

The baby is:

- an object for the care of 'the best mother in the world';
- an individual who runs away;
- a nuisance;
- possessor of a genuine sense of humour.

Because of these variations, the role of the baby is popular. The shared illusion of the play can be maintained even when the baby becomes difficult and demanding. When pretending to be a baby, a child can go through a repertoire of feelings from dependence to rage, from the fear of abandonment to humorous foolery.

Is Dad at home? Are there big brothers in the play? ■

Mothers, big sisters and genderless children seem to populate the home in the girls' playing. (In Finnish there is only one word for he and she. During play children often talk about a baby or a child, but unless they mention the first name or call her or him a boy or a girl, you never know the gender.)

Fathers

However, the families are not totally fatherless. Some girls talk about fathers and big brothers in their 'family' play, especially when this kind of pretend play takes place outdoors. So, what do fathers and big brothers do?

Traditional roles for fathers

Tiia tells us, somewhat vaguely, that fathers cut wood 'with an axe or a hammer' and big brothers go to the shop. Anu explains: 'They always come after food . . . and otherwise they go to war.' It is hard to keep men indoors at home! They search for roles with more action and more space. Outdoors it is easier for boys to act the way they naturally do i.e. moving about more, and using a wider space than girls.

Cutting wood puts fathers into a traditional role stereotype, although the interpretation is somewhat shaky. The role of big brother is partly like the shopping role of big sister – at least from the perspective of a girl.

Boys' play

What do the boys play in between returning 'home' for meals cooked by the girls?

Boys who are, according to the girls, interested in war and fighting give an interesting picture of the 'family' play that they share with girls. Seen from the girls' perspective, the roles of boys are solved in a satisfactory way when they appear home once in a while to have their meals as fathers and brothers. Otherwise, as far as they are concerned, they can do as they want. When fathers and brothers leave the home, they can construct their roles following their own interests without disturbing the life of mothers and children. It would be interesting to know if the boys would describe this play as war play when they return 'home' to where the girls are making food.

Playing as car mechanics – the equivalent of the girls' turtle play?

It seems that boys and girls interpret the same play very differently. In another example, with three boys, they do not go home to get their meals. Instead, they act in an expanded home environment, the garage (Figure 6.2).

Boys play in the sand pit and pretend they are in a parking place:

Petri: I have to change the winter tyres.
Aapo: I already did.
. . .

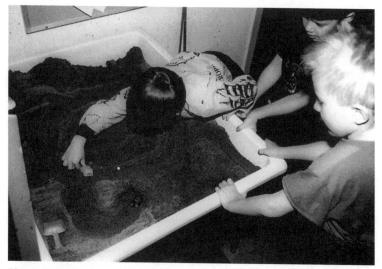

Figure 6.2 'This one drives too fast . . .' When boys play with cars they tank up, change tyres and make a new parking place.

Aapo: Now I use 99 (petrol).
Antti: I prefer diesel.
Aapo: OK, it's turbo-diesel.
Antti: No, it doesn't even exist!
. . .
Petri: I am working and working.
Antti: So am I.
Aapo: It's midnight but I'm working like a fool.

Here, the boys use their play theme as well as the girls in their play with turtles:

- They use their own experiences and their knowledge of the real world as material in their play.
- The narrative structure of the play also resembles the structure of the girls' play with turtles. There is no clear plot with a turning point and climax. The playing starts wherever it can, and ends in the same way.

But the differences in the 'emotional speech' of the girls and the boys is striking. The boys' dialogue is laconic. Even when there is a crash, the same way of talking goes on, and no one screams when someone hurts himself. The approach is pragmatic. There are winter tyres for winter, and summer tyres for summer. Boys work 'like fools' but not a word is said about tiredness.

Rather than dwell on whether this should be defined as boys playing houses, it is more interesting to pay attention to the way in which boys use their own lived experiences in their play. In the girls' play describing human relationships and emotions is so central that concrete events sometimes seem secondary. In the boys' play, changing winter tyres is everything.

The boys' play in the sand pit:

- constructs their future life as a man;
- takes things as they are without sentimentalizing;
- cutting wood, in the war, or in the parking place, boys do not get closer to home than this with the exception of getting their meals.

Girls, for their part, are emotionally at home in their play: the inner experience is often an essential part of the play. Even when girls play with cars, they construct their play in a different way to boys. In Maija's car play, cars are 'boy cars' and 'girl cars'. Even when she is in the street, her parents report that Maija is able to tell the sex of cars. Riikka places small cars tightly side by side. Only the black car is separated from the others. 'One is mother and all the rest are children . . . that one is father . . . Dad is stupid, he does not like others. He does not like children or adults.'

Playing reflects the child's real life

Solo play reflects the private thoughts and feelings of a child

The starting point of the play may reflect the inner life of the child and show what is essential in it. Through her play with cars, Riikka describes her home situation. Because she plays alone, she does not have to explain anything to anybody. (Riikka's mother confirms what we can see: 'Yes, in our family Dad has always been distant, just as he is here.')

Sometimes home play reflects very faithfully the real-life situation of players. When playing alone, Riikka deals with her relationship to her father. While playing with Miia, the two girls go through their shared narrative of growing up.

Towards playing houses as comedy

When Sanna, who is already 9, directs the playing houses, it resembles a comedy where the roles have consciously been created to contrast with each other, and appeal to the sense of humour of the players. Two of the three players are already 9 and they have most probably reached a point in their play where they want to protect their innermost feelings and instead create funny roles like the one of the wild baby.

These examples of playing family show that there are many variations on the same theme, from going through individual experiences to imitating and reconstructing culturally shared role stereotypes.

Finding a shared wavelength for play together

It is sometimes difficult for children to get on the same wavelength in their play. Agreeing a play theme, such as playing families, may not do the trick. There could, quite simply, be completely different home experiences for each child, who may have little in common with the others.

Maija explains the difficulties of this sort of constraint in playing together:

> Whenever we go to Tampere, we stay with a family where the Mum does not work and there is always a girl there called Mari. We always have to find a game and then she always wants to play houses and it is almost always 'houses' and I could not always play 'houses'.

'Houses' is often the first choice, but it does not always work as a shared theme in play. There are many 6-year-old girls who, like Maija, 'could not always play "houses" '. Maija's statement signals both reluctance and at the same time willingness to understand why Mari is so enthusiastic about playing houses and why she cannot share this enthusiasm.

Mari's mother does not work. This may explain why Mari always wants to play houses. For Maija the role of 'home mother' is not familiar. Maija's mother is a teacher in a polytechnic in another city and this is why she is only partly at home on weekdays. There is little common material for play although both of the girls are aged six and have the same cultural background.

Where are the dolls?

One of the most common reasons why children might have a reserved attitude towards playing houses is that it is seen by the children themselves as childish. Certainly, many 6-year-old girls in Finland consider playing with dolls to be childish.

There seems to be a decline in the status of dolls in children's play. The most stereotyped image of playing houses shows girls with their dolls (Figure 6.3). The most traditional childhood memories tell about beloved dolls and faithful doll mothers.

In this chapter, we have seen that the richest examples of girls playing family are not with dolls but with turtles. The girls often play, taking on the roles of characters themselves, rather than using dolls as characters. Where are the dolls in the play of children today?

Baby dolls or Barbie dolls?

In Sanna's bedroom there is a big baby doll sitting on a chair. A moustache and beard have been painted on its face with a felt pen. Sanna does not play with Taneli any more because 'it is too childish'.

Figure 6.3 Homeplay in Pääskylä kindergarten. The somewhat artificial composition reveals how kindergarten teachers wanted to see the children play. At the same time, it is 'true'. It happened that children played in this way.

MK: What do you mean when you say that it is too childish?

Sanna: Hm, I'm already so big, so I don't like that kind of doll any more.

MK: OK, what do you play with then?

Sanna: Barbies sometimes and . . .

MK: I'd still like to ask you, when you said that the doll is so childish what do you think, are there some 6-year-olds who still play with dolls?

Sanna: They have all finished, see, we have changed groups [at the day-care centre].

Sanna contrasts childish baby dolls for small children with Barbies for big children. The statement 'all have finished' defines playing with baby dolls as something suitable for children under six. Greta Pennell (1996) emphasizes, like Sanna, that age is a crucial factor when children choose their toys. Sometimes it is even more important for children to stand out from younger children than it is to be of the opposite sex.

Dolls are no longer seen as human babies to be cared for at all times

In Niina's bedroom there is a big baby doll lying on the floor.

MK: Do you play with the other dolls? . . . you have a big baby doll.

Niina: Yes, I do but sometimes I kick it.

MK: Why do you kick it?

Niina: I kind of want . . .

MK: I mean, for what reason?

Niina: Well, I do not want it to be in my way. There are two more rabbits here . . . oh, where did the little rabbit disappear to?

Niina shows her stuffed animals with enthusiasm, but kicks the baby doll aside when passing it (Figure 6.4). The doll is not a subject for daily care. Kicking it does not mean intentional kicking of *a baby* but rather making space in an indifferent manner. However, the baby doll has lost its status as a human being when it has been lowered to a hindrance on one's way.

In Noora's and Susanna's bedroom I cannot see any dolls at all. This is because they are piled up one upon the other in a deep drawer. Susanna explains: 'I have only given a name to one of them, Salla, because it looked exactly like Salla, but it is my first name . . . I don't

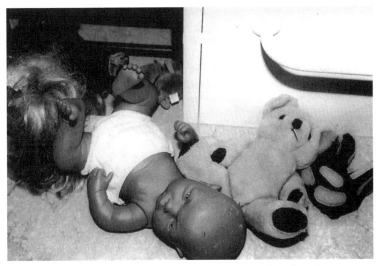

Figure 6.4 Niina's baby doll has been demoted to an obstacle in her way.

like that name.' Another doll is called Little Red Riding Hood 'because her clothes are so red'. Other dolls in the drawer are both nameless and naked.

In Tiia's bedroom I find all her dolls in a corner in doll's pram untouched for a long time. 'Now I am big and big girls don't play with dolls.' Emilia does not have any dolls at all.

When Sanna, Niina, Noora and Susanna play, dolls do not have a central role. Dolls are just another toy, with no special status.

But there are irreplaceable toys that are emotionally meaningful for children. Anu, Emilia, Juuso, Joona and Niina all talk about stuffed animals in this way, rather than dolls. Tiia sighs: 'When I have peace, I remember the old sad things . . . when I lost my teddy bear in the bus and then it was not found. That happened many years ago, so many, that I was three when I lost it.' Emilia reminisces in the same way about her stuffed turtle, which she left in a taxi.

Adults no longer encourage children to have a 'doll child'

The attitude of adults has changed since the 1950s. Few adults would nowadays persistently support a child's play with a 'doll child' who needs care and nurture. At home, in the 1950s, mothers, aunts and grandmothers all supported play with dolls, and the women's magazine, *Kotiliesi* carried an article saying, 'For Christmas, the doll Ulla gets new clothes and it is difficult to know who is enjoying this most, Ulla, her little mother or mother who enjoys sewing the clothes.'

Magazines no longer give patterns for dolls' clothes before Christmas as in the 1950s. It is easier to buy a new doll than make a night shirt or winter coat for the old one. The doll no longer represents a human being (Figure 6.5). Instead the doll is an artefact, with a disposable relationship.

The journalist Tuulia writes in the 1950s in the magazine *Lastentarha* (*Kindergarten*) about 'persons' when talking about dolls and teddy bears:

> I would not call them toys. Maybe they were still toys on the shelves in the shop, serial production, collective mass. But when

Figure 6.5 Toy life in the 1950s and 1960s: dolls as human beings. Dolls were individuals at the kindergarten. Every doll had a name and her own clothes.

they have reached the magic sphere of children they transform to personalities, family members. A child gives them soul from their soul.

The adult's relationship to dolls and teddy bears is described in the same tone:

> Naturally a mother or a grandmother who reminisces about her own childhood, a humorous caretaker or an understanding kindergarten teacher looks at toy persons from a different perspective to the children. The friendship of a child towards a Teddy Bear is different when they prepare clothes, napkins and a sleeping bag from the friendship of the mother or father of the Teddy Bear.

Uncared-for dolls in early years settings

The image of shared play between adult – parents, grandparents, aunts and uncles – and child has faded. Abandoned and uncared-for dolls, nameless and naked are now part of play culture in Finnish day-care centres as well as in children's bedrooms. Naturally, both at home and at the day-care centre we can find dolls who are well looked-after and have names – but this is not the norm as it used to be in the 1950s. A naked and uncared-for doll was an impossible sight in Finnish kindergartens until the 1970s (Figure 6.6). It was the adult's duty to take care of dolls' equipment and to participate in washing and mangling of the doll clothes and bedclothes. In this way the model of a caring mother was transferred to children (Finne 1992).

Birgitta Olofsson (1993) wonders why staff members at Swedish day-care centres do not ask children the name or the age of a doll and why they do not pick up the naked doll lying on the floor in order to show how to make a nappy of paper towels or how to dress it warmly.

Doll play takes place – but alone and at home

Although doll play has lost status as a public kind of play in Finland, by the time the children are 6 years of age, many girls still play with dolls in the privacy of their own homes, if they are alone. 'Anu often pretends that she is the mother of her dolls. Riikka plays with her dolls at home. Jaana says there is still place for a new doll in her doll's pram. Emmi dreams of having a *Baby Born* doll.'

Figure 6.6 Toy life in the 1990s: dolls as 'things' in a Finnish day-care centre.

When so many 6-year-old girls say they 'have all finished' with doll play, this is not true, but it does show the understanding 6-year-old girls have about the cultural norm concerning doll play. None of the girls gives a different view, despite the fact that when girls like Emmi, Riika and Anu begin to describe their own individual play, a picture of doll play at home begins to emerge. Playing alone at home is the way children can safeguard themselves from being labelled childish.

Was doll play as prevalent as we think in the 1950s?

Is it justified to characterize the majority of 6-year-old girls in the 1950s as doll mothers? It is difficult to draw a detailed picture of the situation based on written references. Paavo Päivansalo (1952) for example, states that playing houses is common but on the other hand 'home play does not occur among girls as often as one could expect'. Unfortunately it is as difficult to evaluate the extent that was expected as the norm. Nevertheless it is possible to trace some changes of directions in doll play by looking for:

- the stage when some of the girls stopped playing with dolls;

- the way some of them gradually left dolls behind;
- the way some of the girls still actively play with dolls.

This is a period when girls begin to use pejorative nuances when talking about playing with dolls. Playing with dolls is seen as childish whereas not playing with them is seen as a part of the admirable role of being a big girl. This stage of transition starts earlier today than some decades ago, when some kindergarten teachers reported that playing houses was so popular that four home corners were built in the kindergarten to meet the needs of the children (Finne 1992).

Many girls played with their dolls until they were 11 or 12-years-old so that finding doll play childish was certainly foreign to children under school age. In spite of this, it is true, of course, that individual differences always bring diversity. Even in the 1950s, there were girls who preferred other activities to doll play but the reason was not hurrying to become 'big' but simply that they had other interests.

How play reflects children's understanding of the relationships between men and women

In children's play the relationship between a man and a woman exists side by side with that of a mother and a child. Happy and unhappy love inspires play where the topics are marriage, going to balls and suicide.

Weddings

Emmi enjoys planning Barbie's wedding:

> I am going to play alone at home. I have just got a male Barbie, Ken, and I have not played with it yet, so tonight I am going to play their wedding.

The wedding ceremony has been prepared carefully. Barbie's wedding ring, the wedding crown and the wedding dress have been ready in a box for a long time. The groom, 'man Barbie', Ken:

> is actually such a butterfly prince, so there will be a kind of butterfly wedding issue, the flower bouquet, there is a butterfly and a violet flower or a flower of the colour of a bright lingonberry.

Emmi has attended a wedding ceremony and is going to organize Barbie and Ken's wedding more or less in the same way:

> First, it was so that they kneeled there in front of the priest . . . and they had a black car and they had nice cans and such a string to which they were attached and then we went to a place where we celebrated the wedding. It was fun when they started to dance there. And the cake was wonderful. There were the bride and the man on the top of it. It was nice, it was a wonderful cream cake, strawberry cream cake.

The dream world of Barbie combined with Emmi's own experiences of a wedding ceremony create the framework for this play scenario, and she is looking forward to it. In play acting Barbie and Ken's wedding, this 6-year-old can define the amount of happiness and grasp the endless love between a man and a woman.

In play, children can construct a great drama about love

The play scenario 'suicide on the playground slide', we shall see, is a contrasting play scenario to the wedding scenarios. Relationships between men and women may mean total disaster or consummate happiness. The two play scenarios also contrast in the way play material is used.

In the Barbie and Ken wedding scenario, the narrative is created while the play acting proceeds: the play is neither a pure imitation of the Barbie brochures nor of the summer wedding that Emmi attended. Although Barbie and Ken are 'ready-made' in many senses, play acting always demands continuous invention by the player. The guests have to be found from what is available in Emmi's bedroom. The altar and the dinner have to be constructed from material that is found at home.

Suicide on the playground slide

Suicide on the playground slide is played by two girls, Henna and Emilia. The two girls are conscious that love can become a destructive power, but in this case it is surprisingly the one who has had too much of love who commits suicide, and not, as is usual, the one who suffers from unrequited love.

Henna: One of us is a man and the other one is a woman. And then the woman falls in love with the man. And then the woman runs after the man all the time.

Emilia: And then the man jumps onto the playground slide and we pretend that it is a waterfall and he commits suicide.

MK: What?

Henna: Suicide.

MK: Yes, but what do you pretend the playground slide is?

Henna: A waterfall ... so he jumps down and then the woman starts to cry when he has committed suicide.

Emilia: Then he survives and then the woman runs after him again.

Henna: Then, when daddy, no, the man faints, this woman calls the doctor: 'Help doctor, doctor, help!'

MK: Very exciting, but why does the man want to commit suicide?

Emilia: See, because he doesn't love the woman.

Henna: And doesn't want to see her because he is so fed up with her.

Suicide on the playground slide is a simplified pair relationship drama, where the roles are extremely reduced. The plot is crystallized down to the minimum of events:

1 chase
2 jump into the waterfall
3 panic
4 reviving
5 chase.

A further reduction of the play scenario could change it to 'suicide tag', a simple and repeatable chasing game, or to a dramatic version of 'kiss tag' where girls try to chase boys. However, the original version is without doubt a piece of make-believe play. The girls are fascinated by a love story that ends with a suicide.

Henna and Emilia explain that they got the idea for the story 'from their own head'. Thus it remains unclear what kind of information and impressions form the starting point for this kind of condensed pair relationship tragedy. The only thing that is clear is that children construct their ideas of adulthood using different fragments. The dream and nightmare world of television lives side by side with the everyday life of children and their families.

Perhaps 6-year-olds are not experts in love affairs but their interest in them is vivid. Love and passion occupy their mind. Emilia sadly sings 'an adult's song' that she has learned from her mother:

I walk alone, my dear is dead, the whole town is dead, the birds' song has died down. I loved that man so, his mouth, his eyes, his hands, his heart. There is only sorrow now, only sorrow now.

Although girls do not have to grieve over lost darlings in reality, love is, in accordance to its nature, complicated.

Boy friends and girl friends

Girls talk about their 'boy friends' very straightforwardly.

Tiina: Did you know my boy friend is Mikke? Actually, Mikke does not like me but I like him.

Anu: I already have a boy friend, Joona and Olli too a bit. I don't know which one of them is better.

Tiia is sure about her feelings:

Tiia: I have sometimes kissed Miika, although we did not play it [kiss tag], but Miika ran away when I tried to kiss him because I loved him, because I love him. I would like to get married with him.

Miia: Well, do.

Tiia: I do not know if he wants with me – but you don't have to get married to anybody if you don't want to.

Only Sanna feels uncomfortable when other girls tease her about boy friends and says that she does not have a boy friend.

Girls talk about boy friends. They try to chase them in kiss tag, pretend dating, falling in love, dance with them at balls and weddings – and pretend there is suicide on the play ground slide. Girls are active in their play about relationships between men and women, and their emotional speech flows.

Barbie is not just a 'doll'. 'Big girls' who have finished playing with dolls play with Barbie who is a role model for the future. Girls are reaching out towards being teenagers and adulthood. Play that is about love and passion offers new roles, as well as playing houses, and partly replaces it.

Was this kind of make-believe play present in the 1950s?

Did themes about love, weddings, suicides and boy friends occur in the play acting of 6-year-olds in the 1950s? Is it likely that some

6-year-olds generated these kinds of play ideas 'out of their own heads'?

Because comparable research material does not exist, we can only say that children's experiences, and the fantasy ideas and stories of the era were different from today. The generation of children in the 1950s were, on the whole, living without television, and so they based their play scenarios on the images of adult life according to what they saw adults do in their daily activities. Children attended weddings that were without doubt as impressive as today, but the endless chewing over pair relationships in television was totally non-existent.

The influence of television on children's play culture

The age segregation that is so typical of today does not manifest itself when children are watching television despite the division into children's and adults' programmes. Today, girls watch the same family series as their mothers. They absorb impressions from programmes where human relationships are discussed endlessly. The television connects generations:

> Elderly people and children like to watch the same television programmes in the evening and there hasn't been any dispute about the channels because the favourite programme of both children at the day-care centre and the inhabitants of the home for elderly people is 'Bold and Beautiful'.
>
> (*Helsingin Sanomat*, 15 Sept. 1998)

According to the newspaper, watching the same programme with elderly people is a positive experience for children. No one requires programmes better suited for children. Without doubt, this offers material for children reaching out towards the life of a teenager or adult, and they incorporate it into their play scenarios.

Questions for reflective practice

- Have you noticed how children talk to each other in their make-believe play?
- Have you observed family themes? Do they correspond in any ways to those described in this chapter?
- Consider the gender aspects of the make-believe play of the children you spend time with.

• Have you noticed children developing make-believe play themes about adult love, or do you avoid this? Is this important?

Further reading

Bruce, T. (1991) *Time to Play in Early Childhood Education*. London: Hodder and Stoughton.

Bruce, T. (2004) *Developing Learning in Childhood*. London: Paul Chapman Publishing.

Gussin-Paley, V. (1981) *Wally's Stories*. Cambridge MA: Harvard University Press.

Isaacs, S. (1930) *Intellectual Growth in Young Children*. London: Routledge and Kegan Paul.

7

THE WORLD OF MAKE-BELIEVE 2: PLAY SCENARIOS THAT ARE ABOUT HAVING 'ADVENTURES' AND FIGHTS

Adventures differ from 'normal' life, and adventure play is different from other kinds of play acting. Adventure play does not imitate everyday life, daily events at home that we looked at in the previous two chapters. Instead, it consists of episodes that together form a whole, a narrative with a beginning and an end unlike the stream of small events, with no real beginning or ending that we found in family play. An adventure can be funny, full of surprises, exciting, big or small. An adventure can contain everything that is crucial in life, such as love and hate, courage and cowardice, fighting and submission.

An adventure in the amusement park

Sanna and Tiia pretend they are two kittens. Both of them are called 'Tassu' which means 'Paw'. Sanna says, 'Mum allowed them to go to "Lintsi" (the amusement park) and these kittens got lost and decided to go for adventure and never return home.' In this story Mum allows her children to leave for the amusement park of Linnanmäki, but they lose their way and embark on a forbidden adventure. 'Never return home' is the ultimate decision and is therefore dramatic.

In play children are courageous enough to wander far from home:

- leaving home;
- getting lost;
- endless wandering;
- which takes the players further in the direction away from home.

Children can tell themselves a story of departure in order to examine how it feels to be the one who leaves. The moving away and returning back home that was seen in the turtles play are here replaced by exploring only one direction – away from home – and because the play was interrupted by rain, 'then it started to rain and we went under the playground slide under shelter', we will never know if the story would still have ended with the kittens returning home.

An adventure in wonderland

Emmi, Maria and Ilmari play outside the fence of a small playground. Maria is an egg. Emmi is angel princess on a terrible dragon mountain impossible to escape from. Ilmari is a fairy prince. His first task is to free the angel princess. After he has liberated the princess they leave together for a long wandering which ends in finding an egg. After a long wait, a foal is hatched from the egg.

Emmi: Hi, I would give you this so that you would run like a horse and neigh like a horse.
Maria: I would have been a horse's egg.
Emmi: We have to take a rope.
Maria: I'll go and ask.
(Maria returns after a moment and the play goes on.)
Maria neighs: Ihahhaa! You would notice that I am so wild that you should tie me up now when I'm in place.
Emmi: Let's leave quickly before they come here! Maria, don't move now, I will bridle you! I would quickly leave with a horse.

Katariina joins the play when it is at its best. She becomes the queen. She is left alone to guard the castle which means going around the outdoor play shed. This task is satisfying only for a moment: 'Give me something else to do, so that I don't just have to circle . . . why always around, I get hot!' When there is nothing better to do, the queen quits, saying she is sweltering, and the play goes on with the three players.

Talking with the children about their play

In the afternoon we talk about the morning's play. The framework and plot of the play become clearer as Emmi and Maria talk:

Emmi: Yes, it was a wonderland and a princess was born of an old queen and the princess became queen, and that queen gave

birth to Ilmari (the fairy prince) and then I was such a . . .
that had come from heaven. It was a real angel but it was
named angel princess. Then the play began so that the egg
appeared from heaven. It appeared from the master of the
heaven of the bad spirit . . . and then, hm, I was not with the
bad spirit, the bad spirit put me down on the earth in jail and
then the prince saved me . . . Maria can tell . . .

Maria: And then she wandered a long time and then . . .

Emmi: Riding on a horse!

Maria: No, well, then, she found this egg and then . . .

Emmi: When she rode a horse!

Maria: And then it hatched from the egg . . . and became a horse . . .
but it couldn't gallop and it learned rather quickly and won a
horse race when all the other horses stumbled at the first
obstacle . . . fell into . . .

Emmi: Mud.

Maria: Yes, into a muddy puddle and it could clear all the
obstacles . . .

Emmi: Yes, and they didn't get used to it because they thought it
wasn't fun at all when they had to clear stones and all
kinds of muddy puddles and trees, a terribly high tree, a
tree that was one hundred metres high, it could even clear
that.

Maria: It had trained.

Emmi: Now it is Ilmari's turn to tell.

Ilmari: I don't know so much, the girls talked awfully much.

The prince of the fairy land lets the girls talk and Emmi makes the
essential nature of the egg clearer:

> Yes, it was an egg of a gentle horse queen, who had been a real
> queen, but the evil spirit killed it and the egg when it was born –
> it was a flying horse – so when it flew, it passed the castle of the
> evil spirit and the egg was born then and rolled in front of the
> door of the castle.

'The egg of the flying horse' is a pretend play scenario where the
players create an illusion, a make-believe land where the players,
deeply involved in their roles, wander from one adventure to another
and invent scenes in the story they share.

A shared illusion is an indispensable condition for the play but
probably the children do not share the imaginary world totally. This
is because it is hard to move your inner images into the mind of
someone else. But somehow this happens. It is essential that Emmi,

Maria and Ilmari go out in search of adventure in a make-believe land that is approximately the same for each of them.

How the children play together

During the play acting Emmi directs and constructs a shared orientation, using storytelling language to tell the others the plot of the story she has in mind. However, Maria doesn't wait for Emmi's 'she would say' lines. Instead, she invents her own lines, which makes Emmi take the next step in accordance with them.

Ilmari is also involved in the play but his role is different. He follows the meandering story of the girls, but he does not create anything new.

Katariina never gets into the make-believe scenarios, and she disengages from the play as easily as she joins it. The other players have an indifferent attitude towards Katariina. She can join the play if she wants to but they do not try to bind her in the play because she is not necessary to the plot. Emmi, Maria and Ilmari are in the leading roles, Katariina is only in a minor role.

A complex plot develops – with classic story features

The plot is so complicated, with all its sub-plots, that the players must tolerate a great deal of inaccuracy. But the main idea seems to be clear to Emmi and Maria. The egg of the flying horse has to be found and rescued, and the foal that will hatch from the egg has to be trained into a hero horse admired and envied by everybody.

There are elements of classical fairy tales in 'Angel princess and the egg of the flying horse'. Like many fairy tales, the 'title person', angel princess, has a mission to fulfil and this mission makes it worth suffering and struggling against all kinds of afflictions. The narrative proceeds the way a story does. Problems and their solutions take turns and lead towards the climax of the play and finally to the end of the story.

This narrative is about winning through difficulties and fears (see Bettelheim 1975; Fiske 1987). The angel who is declared angel princess wanders without fear in order to rescue the egg of the flying horse. The climax follows after many adventures. The descendant of the flying horse jumps incomparably as if it had wings, clearing the highest obstacles. And they live happy ever after.

Who inhabits the world of make-believe?

Many adventures of 6-year-olds take place in the land of make-believe. The story is peopled with traditional figures like princes and princesses, kings and queens. The opening of Mika's, Sanna's and Miia's play shows the guard and his horse who infiltrate the castle of 'the good ones':

Sanna: We cheated them! Mika was still an enemy and I was the enemy horse, but then one day at dawn they found out that we were enemies . . . and Mika died and then this horse went to call the princess . . . Miia was princess and the hut was the grave . . . and he did not die in the grave but lay on the floor, and then Mika kind of walked to the hut that had changed to a grave.

The make-believe land of the 'guard play' is darker than the one of angel princess. The revelation of the evil guard is the turning point of the story, and means that goodness wins over badness. In spite of this the dark shades are marked because the roles of the evil ones are central in this play, unlike many other play scenarios where children imagine their enemies because there are not enough players, or because nobody wants to identify with the evil ones who are doomed to fail.

Here, children experience what it is like to be bad and to fail. 'One day at dawn' everything is lost and the evil one who has disguised himself as a guard dies. In play one can face the dark sides of oneself. The experience is meaningful because by identifying with the character and putting one's soul into the role, the feeling is real.

Combinations of real world and fiction in children's make-believe

It is also possible to create the framework of the play by combining the real world with the fiction. For example, the concern for pollution of the sea and the knowledge 6-year-olds have about the food chain may serve as material for playing. The leading role of Emmi's and Maria's play is 'a wise little fish' who helps with 'the pollution of the sea'. For a moment the situation is critical because 'the rabbit didn't produce food and the dolphin didn't. Neither of them produced food.' Finally, all of them fell asleep, weak as they are with hunger.

The climax of this play scenario is the revival of all the sleeping animals. 'As far as I remember, I woke up the flower by spraying it like rain.' The girls have already forgotten some of the details of the play that was invented, and played it only once, but the plot is still clear. The great revival is as impressive as in the story of 'Sleeping Beauty' or in *The Lion, the Witch and the Wardrobe* by C.S. Lewis where the good lion Aslan revives the Narnian people who have been turned into stone statues by the White Wizard.

When children construct their own role, it is possible to combine knowledge with fantasy

> Then we played that I was a magic flower . . . and then it [a turtle] ate its roots, because it did not want to have the roots . . . but because it was a magic flower, it could sing and walk, it did not die, if only it was watered in the middle of the stalk and up and down, because it was such a magic flower it did not need roots, because its roots made weeds grow.
>
> Maria

A rootless flower is a magic flower to one who knows that roots are indispensable for a flower, and the idea of a rootless flower very much amuses Maria. The most beautiful flower in the world that can sing and walk is a fascinating role to create. The magic flower is surrounded by an aura of independence and freedom.

The pretend play about a cockatoo and a hedgehog is about stealing of eggs.

Jonna: My hedgehog took eggs from the cockatoo and . . .
Noora: They were unhygienic, that's why they had blue shells!
Jonna: Yes, there were small chickens and the hedgehog ate them.
Noora: Yes, the shells and all.
MK: What happened next?
Jonna: The hedgehog just lived as before . . . its favourites were embryo eggs!
Noora: Monster embryo eggs!
Jonna: It hoped that all the eggs would be embryo eggs, every one of them!

This fable follows a familiar and simple pattern. One thing tries to seize something from another. But this simple and lifelike play, where a hedgehog eats eggs, becomes more fascinating when eggs are not ordinary eggs but unhygienic monster embryo eggs with blue shells.

How original are the adventure play scenarios that children create?

It is difficult to evaluate how original these adventures are. Children have absorbed the general structure of narrative that is followed in adventure stories. Maria describes their play scenarios as 'invented totally by ourselves'. But there are quotations from stories that children have heard or seen, such as when children try to find the magic slabs of the 'pirates of the old days'. Emmi explains that magic slabs are wanted because the one who has such a slab has ten wishes that will be fulfilled.

Principally, children are able to distinguish between their own play ideas and those that come from other sources. Kalle says, 'Well, I don't know how others find ideas, but I have invented ideas from television and books and sometimes out of my mind.' Emmi, Maria, Emilia and Henna report that they gather play ideas 'from one's own head' and 'from my brain'.

Even when the starting point for adventure play is a story known by everybody, the implementation of it may vary. At the day-care centre Hilapieli children play The Lion King in the skating rink. Sanna describes their play idea: 'Yes, Juuso was Lion King but then it all was spoilt when Miia said that he dies. The Lion King dies, but in the play he did not die, it was another kind of Lion King.'

Rewritten stories show play cultural competence

If someone does not understand a 'rewritten' Lion King, it causes big problems and can even spoil the play. Play cultural competence is also about ability to modify the plot at the crucial points.

Sometimes the idea is to play, as Emmi puts it, 'the right way'. When this is the case the threat for play is the child who does not follow the original manuscript written by an adult. In these accurate re-enactments of stories, it is necessary to know the story. Knowing the story may even be a condition for participation:

Riku: Only those who have watched are allowed to enter the play.
MK: Only those who have watched?
Riku: Yes, because you have to know what they are and what happens, what part we are playing.

On the whole, television adaptations are familiar to everybody, but Sanna and Jonas pointed out that occasionally the plot of an adventure is told so that favoured play-pals are able to participate in the play even if they have not seen the programme that ought to be known by everybody.

When children play alone they can make their own decisions as they play

When Emmi wants to play 'Peter Rabbit' at home, she starts by watching a Peter Rabbit video. She uses figures that are as 'correct' as possible. She has got Peter Rabbit and also 'the terrible uncle'. She has not got the house. She uses a sofa turned upside down as the house. 'Also the cabbages are not real, they are my green blouses . . . I put them like this in lines.'

When children like Emmi play 'in the right way', they try to imitate the original story as exactly as possible. However, children still have to adapt the story in their play. In fact, they have a lot to do. When children act 'in role', they have to find out the way these roles are carried out. Sometimes they have to find play props so that they can carry out the play in the way they want to.

When a child plays alone, the whole physical environment serves as a store house for props which can then be used creatively in their play. The sofa becomes a house. The green blouses become cabbages.

The children's ideas are mixed with borrowed ideas in many ways in this kind of play acting. Universal and timeless fairy tales and other narratives tell stories about people. The essence of human nature is crystallized in these stories. The same themes are available for children to use in their play. Children tell themselves stories about themselves through these archaic narrative structures, themes and variations of them.

Good guys and evil guys – one or the other! ∎

Power Rangers

When boys take part in play scenarios involving fighting, they are on one of two sides, good or evil. There is no ambiguity about this. They are either good or bad. Boys play Power Rangers. The starting point is a television series where Rita, the mistress of the evil, fights with her followers against Zordon, the good magician, and the Power Rangers.

In real life, the 'goodies' are teenagers who go to school, but when they transform into Power Rangers, they are pulled into unbelievable fights against the super bastards of Rita. Every one of the five youngsters has an identifying colour which corresponds to their dominating characteristics. All of them are good at karate but in the first place their force is based on 'the ability' given to them by Zordon, to transform to effective Powerzord fighting machines, the model of which are dinosaurs that governed the earth during a prehistoric era, but equipped with more modern weapons.

Tuomas directs the play in the big hall of the day-care centre. Tuomas, Petteri and Juho are good guys, Red, Black and Blue. Joni is an evil guy, 'probably Kroko'.

Joni:	He could not move!
Tuomas:	He would laugh . . . and now he would take me and would hang me . . . this would be the end of all of me.
Kroko (Joni):	Hands behind!
Red (Tuomas):	I can't help it . . . I have to.
Kroko (Joni):	I would put fire all around them.
Red (Tuomas):	Everything is lost!
Black (Petteri):	Better not to laugh, soon we will all be dead . . . I am saying my last words.
Red (Tuomas):	Now you can say your last wish . . . And now I say I wish we can be terribly strong!

The brave Power Rangers lie on the floor with hands tied behind their back. The crackle of the fire gets stronger – Kroko piles up mattresses over the boys. The tension gets unbearable – does evil win? At the last moment the Power Rangers transform, they gain supernatural strength and manage to escape from being burnt at the stake. Tuomas says, 'I took such a hard issue, so Zordon heard it and then he gave me terribly much strength and then I destroyed those bars.'

The dramatic final scene is the climax of this Power Rangers play. Before this, the Power Rangers have managed to solve many critical situations – but not easily, because as Tuomas explains, 'otherwise this playing is not exciting at all'. The excitement is based on fighting, fleeing, getting caught, being shut in jail and narrowly escaping (Figure 7.1). Technical problems cause unexpected situations that lead into knotty problems. Now and then the game seems to be up. Tuomas says, 'They stay here for ever' or 'first they fry them and then they will eat them'.

These boys watch *Power Rangers* regularly, and so the theme of the play is familiar to everybody. In spite of this, the play, which lasts for an hour, is not just a matter of repeating what everybody already knows. The role of director of the play falls to Tuomas, and is especially challenging. He directs, has star billing and 'writes the manuscript' at the same time. The others act according to role expectations.

Figure 7.1 Power Rangers in jail. Fortunately they have stomachs full of rolls and rye crisps.

The play makes one think of the first rehearsal of a play without an audience. What makes the difference is that children play this scenario for its own sake.

Improvising a play scenario script

This story, with the four characters taken by the boys, demands an improvised script which organizes the play acting:

Kroko (Joni):	You will become steak very soon!
Tuomas:	No, Kroko should come here first and say 'You will soon!'
Kroko (Joni):	(Moves to the right place.) 'You will soon become steak!'
Tuomas:	Just because of this he would hit him on his balls, and he would say 'Aaah'!
Petteri (Black):	Aaah!
Tuomas:	Now he would put this kind of issue on him so that they would revenge . . .

Tuomas keeps the play going through the script he improvises. He organizes, directs and corrects what the others do. At the same time he constantly moves between the fantasy world of play and the 'real' world. Popping in and out of the real world is necessary in this kind of play but it also prevents a total involvement in the play acting. This is why the most intense moments of *flow* are seen when the players share the reality of the play totally. Then the play and the players are the same. In this play the *flow* is reached with tense excitement before the final scene.

Ancient themes in stories – the battles between good and evil

Tuomas has a real sense of drama. He directs his group through small difficulties to small victories and finally through a big difficulty to a great victory. In so doing he repeats an archaic narrative theme. However, in between the furious adventures there are also peaceful moments. While in jail, Petteri (Black) sighs for home: 'Oh wasn't my own bed at home so much better than the one in this cell.' Tuomas (Red) gives some background information to Kroko (Joni): 'He would think that the Power Rangers don't have food.' Blue (Juho) answers in a Finnish way: 'I would munch a roll . . . would go to Zordon to get one rye crisp, lots of rye crisps.' However, the local detail is quickly followed by a new turn that makes the plot proceed: 'Now the guard would notice that our stomachs are terribly full.'

After this play acting Tuomas reflects on the story of Power Rangers further. 'Maybe Rita has developed Power Rangers in the world. I wonder why the evil ones sometimes create an enemy against themselves just in order to give them a reason to fight.' For Tuomas it is not enough to 'just fight'. Good and evil are needed to make the fight meaningful.

Media play

This Power Rangers play is a good example of how the fight between good and evil is dealt with in children's play acting. It is also an example of how supranational mass entertainment influences play; Margareta Rönnberg (1991) calls it 'media play'.

When children's need for play and collectively shared material for play come together, the play goes well. The players can anticipate that everybody knows the basic twists and turns of the plot, but when the playing is at its best, the implementation varies from time to time. The boys do not simply repeat the latest part they have seen but combine episodes they have found exciting in new ways, sometimes with a bit of local spice.

The fight between good and evil – *Biker Mice*

When their home planet, Mars, is on the verge of destruction by the Plutarkians, a bunch of Humanoid Mice escape their world. Throttle, Vinnie, and Modo, a trio of Biker Mice were shot down and crash landed on Earth where they became friends with a human mechanic named Charley.

Biker Mice fight without fear against their enemies Lawrence Limburger, Dr Karbunkle and other Plutarkians. Images of strength and quickness are powerful and almost everything is possible for Biker Mice. Oskari, Jere, Juuso, Jukka and Petri are very clear that Modo is the most wanted role because he has a 'machine hand'.

Jere: Modo can shoot from his hand.
Oskari: Yes, and from his moped and his gun but the gun is not in his hand, he has got weapons, ordinary guns.
Jere: In his hand he has got two weapons in the hatch, two kinds of weapons and then two blue beams come from the hatch.
Oskari: No, one rocket super power and one pistol, an ordinary pistol.
Jere: Yes, and it changes there into a blue beam, you know.
Oskari: Yes, in the air and from the air everybody can see that they are really fine. Then they think that he shoots treasures and then they jump towards him at once but then they will be destroyed.

Modo has managed to turn bad luck in the battle to his victory: he lost his hand but the new 'machine hand' is even better than the original one. He has also become the spiritual leader of Biker Mice although his reputation is based on victories earned through technical qualities.

Heroism and evil characters – who plays what part?

The greatest fulfilment of heroism is experienced by players who act in the role of Red in Power Rangers or as Modo in Biker Mice. There are often long disputes and negotiations about these roles. Rank-and-file heroism is not enough for everybody though it is clear that if you belong to Power Rangers or Biker Mice you are on the winning side.

Enemies are necessary in these games but nobody is forced or pushed to take a role as evil. This is a common rule in all play involving fighting scenarios. Sometimes somebody voluntarily takes the role of an enemy. Mikke is sometimes an enemy 'because I think it is fun to be evil sometimes'. When Joni voluntarily takes the role of Kroko, it means he gets a better role than would otherwise have been offered to him.

The focus during the play is on battles between good and evil, and not on violence. On the whole, nobody wants to be evil. The result is that boys fight against invisible enemies. Invisibility solves the problem of roles that are not wanted but it also removes the risk of being hurt. Jukka explains that 'If there are enemies, we can beat them up, we can do what ever we want!' Rough aggression and brawling are kept in their place during fantasy play. Invisible enemies sustain kicks, beating up, whatever.

Jukka's words reflect the kind of violence that is found in both *Power Rangers* and *Biker Mice*, television programmes that are popular among 6-year-old boys. Yet, it is worth noticing that for all of the boys the talk is mostly about fights between good and evil and not about violent scenes. There are links here with the findings of Penny Holland in an earlier book in this series (2003).

Mixing characters from different television programmes, from Turtles to Batman

At the foot of Mika's bed there is a handful of small plastic figures. There are good guys and evil guys who fight against each other in Mika's folded mountains of quilts. The good guys of popular television series come together and fight for good. There are:

six Turtles
one Biker Mouse (Vinnie)
one Phantom soldier (Freeder)

Anonymous 'army men' are evil guys in these fights. Jesse, Mika, Riku and Tuomas explain that when they are at home, they will use 'mixed groups' of good guys simply because they don't have complete sets of good or bad guys.

At the day-care centre boys act the roles they give their plastic characters at home. Just as the availability of plastic dolls influences the stories played at home, so in the day-care centre, the number of boys available determines the kind of play acting. At the centre, there may not be enough children to make the complete set of Power Rangers or Biker Mice and even if there were, children sometimes prefer to play 'mixed games'. Riku and Petri explain that there could be characters from different television series.

Preparing weapons

Images of fighting also motivate boys to prepare weapons. In many a bedroom one can see a sword skilfully made at the day-centre. Six-year-olds Joni and Petteri are deeply involved in their work by the planning-bench. They choose suitable pieces of wood, take the hammer and nails and make machine guns for themselves. The weapons are tested by shooting the cooker of the day-care centre (Figure 7.2). Preparing the weapon is a part of the game, sometimes even a very important part of it.

Are play fighting scenarios forbidden to girls?

Is the fight between good and evil only boys' business?

Tuomas: Girls don't like Power Rangers, though actually two girls could join the game sometimes . . . but there has not really been any girls.

Juuso: There be more than four in it [Power Rangers play]. There are two girls, Yellow and Pink, in it but no one ever came and we wouldn't like it either.

Figure 7.2 The machine gun is ready. Joni tests his weapon by shooting towards the cooker of the day-care centre.

There are ready-made roles for two girls, Kimberley and Trini, 'but nobody comes'. Tuomas finds that there 'should' actually be girl fighters as well, whereas Juuso thinks that it is possible but not desirable to occupy the vacant roles in the game. The boys have not actually rejected girls who would have liked to be Yellow or Pink fighters but there have not been any girls willing to join boys' play acting.

It is intriguing that when Henna, Emilia, Sanna and Miia talk about their play, they relate that they have sometimes participated in Power Rangers. Sanna was 'an enemy, a spider that spits, shoots slime on others'. These 6-year-old girls talk about how it is possible to create new roles like Sanna being 'a cat of Red or Yellow or Black or . . . you can be a crayfish that eats Baltic herring'. Tiina has joined the play as a turtle mother and baby, though 'actually there are no turtles in the play but sometimes there can be some turtles in it'.

The roles of the girls are minor roles. The spider that shoots slime is aggressive and loves action. That seems to fit well in Power Rangers play. Cats and turtles, on the other hand, do not fit so easily, so they wander on the outskirts of the fighting play, far from the focus of the fight. The roles the girls take resemble the remote roles of the boys in the girls home play, i.e. fathers and brothers with fighting as their hobby.

It is possible to join a play fighting scenario in many ways. The aim might be state of *flow* shared with others or simply the feeling of being together with others. If a girl wants to join the others without being very interested in Power Rangers, she can choose a role that feels her own. She can put her own play ideas into the character of Red's cat.

Girls play different versions of Power Rangers and Biker Mice

When girls play Biker Mice without boys they make a new version of it. Two sisters Noora (6 years) and Susanna (9 years) play with their friend Heli with Biker Mice figures. Susanna says, 'It's not true that there has to be an enemy and a friend. Mostly we don't play it that way. Sometimes we play that someone is very lazy or angry or so but mostly we play with no enemies and they are all friends.'

Without any scruples these girls water down the fight between good and evil and change it into laziness, hatred and friendship. What is more, the war cry of Biker Mice changes in girls' play into a verbal joke. This links with the observations Vivian Gussin Paley has made of children at play.

How children learn about the themes selected for play fighting

Of course, in the 1950s, both *Power Rangers* and *Biker Mice* were unknown. Not all the 6-year-olds knew about Native American Indians or cowboys either. Television was only just entering Finnish homes, and stories about Indians and cowboys were not among the stories that were told or read loud to little boys.

This meant that stories told by older boys were the only way to discover these kinds of stories. It is possible that some play fighting themes started at a somewhat later age than they do now. Naturally the development of literacy skills gradually opened the door for developing new play themes for fighting through cartoons and adventure books.

Although names of characters and the stories change with time, the basic theme remains: the good and the evil fight with each other. The combination is based on stereotypes. Cowboys are good, Indians are bad, Power Rangers good, Rita Repulsa, and her companions, evil.

Marcus Magnusson (1996) finds it strange that children identify themselves with Power Rangers that are roughly stereotyped and simplified figures but he supposes that when a role is simple and unchangeable, it is easier to identify with than a complex character.

On the other hand, when one observes boys' play fighting scenarios and then talks with them about these, it becomes clear that boys are not interested in the 'aesthetics of violence'. Nor are they interested in what we might call the nuanced analysis of the characters of good guys and evil guys. They do not go in for subtle and complex characterizations of their 'goodies' and 'baddies'.

The horrors of real war are remote and unreal. If the confrontation of good and evil is detached, the way girls play it, the point of the play is watered down. Stereotypes are needed to maintain the confrontation between good and evil. The clear polarization justifies the fight. Only when one is completely good and the other completely bad is it possible to fight with pure weapons.

Thus play material with very clear confrontation between good and evil offers the best models for this kind of play acting. The confrontation between bad Indians and good cowboys served as a theme for play in the 1950s. Power Rangers and Biker Mice are themes for today. Power Rangers and Biker Mice are commercial, superficial and stereotyped but in spite of this, their fictional nature has its advantages. The good and evil of these series do not risk the same kind of misunderstandings as play themes in the 1950s, where white cowboys were labelled as good and 'red' Indians as bad. The fact that there were also brave good Indians brought some relief to the situation but did not totally solve the problem of having ethnicity as criteria for being good or bad.

Power Rangers are all good regardless of the colour of their skin. Jason (Red) is white, Zachary (Black) black and Trini (Yellow) Asian. But the question still remains: why is the leader figure white?

Why does the fight between good and evil seem to be an eternal theme?

It is obvious that the fight between good and evil is a central theme in boys' play acting regardless of decade. Six-year-old boys speak consistently and repeatedly about a game they play over and over again. 'I always have good guys and bad guys in my play.' 'That's what I have, too, except when I don't play fighting games.'

Does the theme of eternal fight prove that boys' play acting is one-sided or is there something so essential in the fight between good and evil that it has to be repeated time after time? What story do boys tell about themselves to themselves through this kind of play? Is it about conquering the world and longing for the experience of being hero? Is it essential for growing and for gender identification?

Repetition of a play theme does not mean the play is inevitably low level

Girls' play acting is sometimes considered as more complex and multilayered than boys' play acting regardless of whether they get their impulses from television or from somewhere else. According to Harriet Bjerrum-Nielsen and Monica Rudberg (1991), the girls' play acting is more complex than boys' playing especially before they become 7 years old. After this boys' play acting seems to become more imaginative than that of girls.

Repetition of a theme does not automatically lead to impoverished play in 6-year-old boys. The Power Rangers play, directed by Tuomas, is a good example of this. Repetition also has a meaning.

Children face their dark side during play scenarios

Conquering the world as a good hero is the point of all play fighting scenarios. This kind of play also offers the possibility to try out being the evil guy. But few 6-year-olds are emotionally ready to be the evil guy, who will lose. Only some of the 6-year-boys are able to face their dark side in their play, by taking the burden of absolute evil on their shoulders for a moment.

In the roles children take in their play, children show us what they understand of themselves, and how they see themselves as their sense of self- identity develops. In order to gradually develop a more subtle, multi-layered and nuanced sense of 'right' and 'wrong', children, particularly boys it seems, first need to play at fighting between clearly defined good and evil. This is why the interpretations of some researchers, well acquainted with Power Rangers, seem artificial.

Marcus Magnusson emphasizes:

- the choreographic beauty of violence;
- the fascination of technology;
- the playfulness of incredible fights.

as the secret of long-lasting popularity.

Margareta Rönnberg (1997), however, lashes out at the opponents of *Power Rangers* and has a sarcastic attitude to the concluding words of Swedish television: 'In reality fighting is both stupid and cowardly. Think about it!' She finds the reminder unnecessary because, according to her, *Power Rangers* is not about real fighting. Instead, it is about unbelievable and playful action. Rönnberg finds that *Power Rangers* have a well-established popularity in Swedish playgrounds because children do not think that the fight between good or evil is real.

How the boys see their own play

The interpretation of the 6-year-old boys is different. They put their soul into the play. The inner reality of the play means for them a world where dividing characters into good and evil is:

- the condition for action;
- a way to have control over threatening images.

Thus, they do not claim that they pretend fighting but they fight in a world that exists due to a shared illusion.

Questions for reflective practice ■

- Do the children you spend time with play out adventure themes?
- How do you know this?

- Consider the arguments put forward in relation to themes of good and evil in this chapter. Does this resonate with your observations?
- How influenced is the play by television and electronic media?
- Do you find ancient and classic themes in the play?

Further reading

Holland, P. (2003) *We Don't Play with Guns Here: War, Weapon and Superhero Play in the Early Years*. Maidenhead: Open University Press

Kline, S. (1995) *Out of the Garden. Toys and Children's Culture in the Age of TV Marketing*. London: Verso.

8

FOOLING ABOUT IN PLAY: THE 'DIZZY' SIDE OF PLAY CULTURE

Whirling water

The kind of play that we might call 'dizzy' seems to well up inside us quite naturally. Caillois calls this kind of playing *ilinx*, using the Greek word for whirling water. This is a powerful image.

Children all over the world seem to enjoy swivelling and the feeling of dizziness that comes with it. A momentary need to turn the world upside down and fool about together seems to be a universal phenomenon. Does this mean that this kind of play is independent of culture? It is fascinating to look at children's 'dizzy' play. It is equally interesting to see how adults react to this kind of play.

Swivelling makes you feel lovely and dizzy

Noora and Maija can be seen enjoying a quick swivel round the lamp pole, or twisting the chains of the swing and letting their friend swivel round and round. Swivelling makes Linda feel a lovely dizziness, although 'you are not allowed to twist the chains too high if the other one does not want it'. Jonna describes how 'voluntary dizziness' is wonderful. She says that being forced to become dizzy is awful and not play at all. Petri 'falls' from the table, stiffening himself, and lands on a heap of mattresses (Figure 8.1). Antti and Aapo take turns at doing this too. Now and then boys burrow under the mattresses. It is thrilling to play like this.

Figure 8.1 Falling in a pile of mattresses makes Petri feel dizzy.

Rough play: wild dog play

Wild dog is rough play. The idea is simple. The other dog has to be pushed into liquid lava by fair means or foul. Oskari (6-years-old) is a bulldog. Piia (9-years-old) a holldog. They explain, 'Though such a race doesn't really exist.' These wild dogs attack each other on their parents' water bed!

Oskari: First we have to go to our place.
Piia: It is kind of fighting.
Oskari: Yes, so that one of us can push the other one down over the edge and then we pretend that it is a ravine with lava.
MK: Liquid lava?
Oskari: Yes, and you die at once in a minute!
MK: Even less if it is liquid lava.
Oskari: Yes, but if you can hold the edge of the bed with your hands you won't die, but if your feet . . .
Piia: You die if your feet are in there!

The fighting between the dogs is furious. Bulldog and Holldog swivel around on the bed growling, screaming and panting. The play ends when both are totally exhausted and out of breath.

MK: Are you allowed to do whatever you want to?
Oskari: Yes!
Piia: Yes, you are allowed to kick and bite and tickle.
Oskari: Not bite . . .
Piia: Yes, you are allowed to bite!
Oskari: But we have never bitten.
Piia: No, but once you bit my nose!
Oskari: Yes.
MK: Luckily your nose has recovered.
Piia: Yes.
Oskari: Because I didn't bite with all my strength, I didn't want to
          bite like that, because I was afraid that her nose would be
          broken.

Unrestrained play – but there are boundaries

Wild dog play is about as far as possible from games of competition,
chance or destiny, and the make-believe play we have looked at so far.
Here we see play that involves dizziness, and fooling about. Chaos is
the element that distinguishes wild dogs from the 'real' world. Here
we see a totally unrestrained kind of play acting which reaches a point
of extremity.

Everything seems to be allowed. Oskari and Piia reflect seriously on
the question whether there is anything you are *not* allowed to do. As
we have seen, Oskari has in the middle of the battle, refrained from a
full biting, and in so doing kept the play as play. He kept the bite 'as a
playful bite'. It suggests a real bite, but it's not the same as a real
bite (Bateson 1976).

Piia says, 'Yes we kind of kick almost for real, but we know how to
budge in a way.' The idea is not to hurt the other but there is the need
to become sufficiently free from the rules of the 'real' world for a
moment. This allows physical raging without restrictions – and yet
the boundary between play and reality is still kept in place.

Fighting, playing noisily and chaos: the characteristics of *dizzy* play

Children prefer to give their play a name. 'Pyllyttely' is a fooling
about name for play that invites messing about:

> We've made up 'pyllyttely' with Sini. I take Sini by the bottom
> and Sini tries to bite me with her lips and it's great fun!

Big sister is on all fours and Emilia hangs on her back with two arms around her waist. When Sini tries to catch Emilia with her lips she is like a dog who tries to catch its tail.

Rough and tumble play between parents and their children

The children explain that sometimes it is possible to mess about with their parents in physical and wild rough and tumble play. Mikael and his mother enjoy play 'wrestling' and 'rucksack play'. Mika's father thinks that physical play is important to children. For example, he says:

> Mika and Tiina are sacks in my arms and I throw them, push them, bounce them in bed or then they attack me and we wrestle all the three of us or then we pretend that I am a horse and they try to calm down a runaway horse . . . all kinds of things.

Maija's mother and father both become involved in rough and tumble play. Her mother remembers that 'There was a phase when the playing Maija liked best was tickling or tickling machine.' Her father adds, 'Especially on Sunday morning. We often played that we baked Maija like bun dough, and she would scream, and of course it is also a way to wake up the child so that the child doesn't notice that she has woken up.'

There are gentler forms of dizzy play

In this kind of play, the feeling of getting caught unexpectedly is, for Emilia, part of the charm of playing while her parents are lying in bed sleeping in on a lazy morning. The parents might transform into mountains. The older sister 'opens and closes the mountains' and Emilia says, 'I have been a hedgehog sometimes, and then the hedgehog gets caught in between the mountains.'

When Riikka's mother runs her finger up the child's spine, and lands on the ear, it is called 'Korvanaku' play, because 'korva' is an ear in Finnish. When a different finger 'walks' on Riikka's arm, neck, and back, she and her mother call it 'Rapu' play. Rapu is a crayfish.

If Riikka gets sand in her hair, her mother runs her fingers over her head and they call it 'Sand Rooter' play. 'Hietatonkija', the Sand Rooter is tempted by finding the sand in Riikka's hair, and tries to root it out.

These are gentler kinds of dizzy play that only make you feel a little shiver running down your back.

The differences between competitive play and dizzy play

In the dizzy play explored in this chapter we can see that physical satisfaction wells up in a different way to, say, the physical training involved in learning to play ice hockey. Then the rules are set by adults and the aim is to develop skills that are needed in ice hockey.

Dizzy play is of short duration and is all about swivelling, falling, yielding to the hands of another person when they throw you and send you flying. It means bouncing, tickling, and being bounced about and tickled.

But in wild dogs we can also find elements of make-believe play. Role taking increases the fascination of the dizzy kind of play. We can see that being a bulldog and a holldog as fighting partners, and introducing liquid lava both serve to strengthen the dramatic nature of the dizzy play. When Oskari invites Piia to play wild dogs it is different from simply saying 'let's rage and try to push each other off the water bed'. In spite of age and gender differences, both Piia and Oskari love wild dogs.

Wild women   ■

When children become involved in dizzy play, it's no good if one child tries to talk in the 'real' language of the 'real world'. We can see in the following extract, that takes place in a noisy hall, that Niklas tries to react in a real world way to the aggressive girls who attack the boys, by saying, 'You are not allowed to bark and call us names.' It means he has no point of contact with the boisterous girls. Consequently, his remark is totally passed over.

Two boys, Niklas and Atte have climbed up the sidewall. Toni stands in the middle of the floor, catching girls who are running back and forth from one wall to another.

Juulia starts:	Mira has fallen in love with Toni!
Toni answers:	Juulia has fallen in love with Minttu!
Juulia:	Toni has fallen in love with his own pippeli [child's word for penis].
Minttu shouts:	Pippeliporkkana! [penis-carrot]
Juulia screams:	Toni is falling in love with fresh shit!

Minttu and Juulia go to the sidewall. Now it is Atte's and Niklas' turn.
Minttu roars with laughter: Atte has got tights! Niklas has fallen in love with fresh shit!

Juulia tries to go further: Niklas has fallen in love with his own
                 fart . . .

Minttu: There is a picture on Niklas' socks, do you know
                 what, it is brains resembling a heart!

Juulia examines Niklas' socks: She [the figure on Niklas' socks] looks
                 just like Jasmine [a singer]! Look at Jasmine's tits!

Juulia: There are tits and pimppi [child's word for vagina].

Mira: And you can see Jasmine's bottom!

Minttu shouts: Balls and penis-carrot!

Finally Niklas raises his voice and tries to defend himself. You're not allowed to bark and call us names!

[No one listens to him. Girls run back and forth screaming and
       jumping.]

Juulia comes up with a riddle: Guess what has two tits and fourteen balls?

Mira: Don't know.

Juulia enjoys the moment: Snow White and the seven dwarfs!

The boys escape, but the girls continue the play.

    Girls totally dominate this piece of dizzy play. They join in with Toni's cry, 'Juulia has fallen in love with Minttu!', but that is all they say. They seem to be embarrassed when coarse words fly around them, until finally they simply slide out of the door.

Is there more to what the girls shout than coarse language during their dizzy play?

Although the speech of the girls may seem quite haphazard, in fact, they are all following the same theme closely. As they shout out, they move from 'childish' lavatory language to sexual topics. Six-year-olds are interested in sexuality. Sex pervades the children's world through TV, newspapers and advertisements, as well as directly during discussions amongst their peers.

    Juulia has learned the Snow White joke from a programme that comes on late Saturday night on television. Minttu wonders about the fourteen 'balls', but Juulia tells her what she knows about anatomy, and explains it to her.

Minttu: If I see tits in television, I always do this. [She covers her eyes

with her hands] ... they always make love ... it is
disgusting.

Juulia goes on: Saku has told me that he has seen a film where a man
slightly opened a woman's pimppi [child's word for vagina]
and started to suck it.

MK: So what do you think about it?

Minttu: Nothing.

Juulia: He just told it to me.

Minttu: Now I want Juulia to tell me too.

Juulia: And you have seen someone dig the pimppi of somebody.

Minttu: Yes, but it is a book . . . it is a cat.

Juulia: A cat?

Minttu: Yes, the cat started to dig the woman's pimppi, it is a car-
toon and the woman was a cat.

Juulia laughs.

Minttu: Well, his name is Riz-cat . . . then he starts . . .

Juulia: To dig its own pimppi.

Minttu: No, he licks his lips when he thinks what he would do with
the woman. Then he takes off her shirt, suddenly undresses
it. Then the cat woman does like this. Then he takes her
skirt when the woman is lying down, then he comes like
this, panties down, then he takes all the clothes and throws
them on the floor and starts to dig. He is on his knees with
clothes on.

Naturally, one has to be careful in order to avoid creating a picture of
little girls who have actually seen pornographic programmes and
comic strips. Most of the 6-year-olds have probably not heard about
oral sex, not even from other children. Yet the discussion between
Minttu and Juulia shows what happens when parents are not able to
set clear boundaries, a society saturated with sex and television does
not keep adults' secrets. What Minttu says reflects her ambivalence.
On the one hand, she finds seeing breasts and love-making disgusting. On the other hand, she wants to hear Juulia tell the oral sex scene
again.

Forbidden play

During lunch time at the day-care centre Juulia and Minttu have fun
by naming sexual organs in a loud voice in Arabic. The girls feel a
thrill of excitement when without inhibition they say words that are
forbidden, but not understood by others because they are disguised in
another language. As long as the teachers do not know, they can go on

with their play. They have learnt these words from a friend whose father taught them. Here we see that what one of the fathers has taught his own child reaches other children but not the adults.

Minttu and Juulia are exceptionally interested in sex. Their interest is seen in their play acting and even more strikingly in their speech. However, Minttu and Juulia present a trend that is seen in a less strong form in the play acting and speech of many other 6-year-old girls as well.

These examples shatter the image of children whose sexual interest is supposed to be fumbling and without target (Bjerrum-Nielsen and Rudberg 1991). The intensity of the sexual interest depends on the way sexual material is trickled or poured into the consciousness of a child. It is not surprising that sexual interest once in a while flows out in chaotic dizzy play.

In this kind of play acting children do not imitate adult life in a realistic way. Instead they reach daringly towards issues that adults have forbidden to children because they belong to adult life. They turn pertinence to impertinence, sensitivity to hardness, precociousness to regression. What children cannot symbolize and work out in their minds, bursts out abruptly and out of control.

Play that turns the world upside down

The idea of turning something upside down is part of dizzy play. It often appears in short-lived flashes. We can see this in the 'traffic light game' where the rules are turned upside down. On the wall, there are three cardboard circles, red, yellow and green. Three girls step over the threshold.

> 'Green!' Elina shouts.
> (All the girls cross the street but they return back directly.)
> 'Red!' Emilia shouts.
> (The girls rush into the street and get run over. They fall on each other giggling.)

Rushing into the road when the light is red turns the rule of the road upside down. It becomes a 'message of play' which is at once followed by other girls. A joke is a joke only if the players know rules of the road and so can understand that the joke is based on breaking them.

Dizzy play often takes place spontaneously. When children are involved in any kind of play:

• It might take a new direction and turn into chaotic dizzy play.

- Sometimes one word or one sentence is enough to turn the world upside down.
- Sometimes the playing starts when dad clasps the child in his arms.
- Rough and tumble, dizzy play carries away the players.
- Some games, like wild dogs, have a guarantee of dizziness.

Interestingly players who meet each other during dizzy play are strikingly different. Here we see players of both sexes and of different ages. Sensible big sisters who are seen by adults as 'doing well at school' romp about with their little brothers and sisters. Parents romp with their children – although mothers seem to avoid the wildest dizzy intensity.

Dizzy play: past and present

Dizzy play holds its own across time. When parents let children use their water bed to play wild dogs, or allow their sitting room to become the stage for a raging Power Ranger scene, it shows the permissive attitudes of parents today. Many parents do not want to deny anything unless it is absolutely necessary.

We saw earlier in the chapter that the parents of Sini, Emilia, Mikael, Mika and Tiina, also join with their children in the dizzy kind of play. This shows the wide-ranging roles of parents from conscious 'educator' to participation in wild play.

We can see how adults at the day centre let children use the big hall for dizzy, raging play. When the boys' play becomes too wild, Anne, the nursery nurse, suggests wrestling instead of the unruliness and rough and tumble of the dizzy Power Rangers play.

It is difficult to compare dizzy play across the generations, because situations with capricious and momentary dizzy play have only been documented occasionally. From the writings we do have about play during the 1950s, it seems likely that dizzy play would have been less tolerated than today, especially indoors. This is not to say that adults did not recognize children's need for dizzy play. They did, and they catered for it too.

For example, some kindergartens, such as Ebenseser Kindergarten, where kindergarten teachers were trained, had what was called a daily 'noisy time'. This was in sharp contrast to the other more systematic and controlled activities of the kindergarten. The only rule was that it was forbidden to hurt other children. The biggest temptation of the 'noisy time' was the huge playground slide with 5 metres of shining linoleum which meant that children could slide down it at high speed.

The attitudes of the adults were contradictory. 'Control of the group' was an essential part of the professional skill of a kindergarten teacher. But during the 'noisy time' each day, the idea was to give a maximal release of control. It was not easy for kindergarten teachers to change their orientation so completely at different points in the day, and they often 'lost their nerve' when they looked at children who seemed to be running wild in the hall (Finne 1992).

On the one hand, they felt uncomfortable when the situation seemed to get out of control. On the other, they believed that children had to be able to release their energy after having to sit concentrating on different kinds of tasks led by the kindergarten teacher. The 'noisy time' each day was thought to be a controlled answer to the children's need for uncontrolled action.

Children in the 1950s had opportunities for long periods of play outside in early childhood settings. They had a great deal of freedom for all kinds of play including dizzy play. Nevertheless, dizzy play that might burst out at an inconvenient time was seen as a problem. In the 1950s, this was dealt with in ways which we might expect at a time when parents were more certain of their role, in what, earlier in the book, we have described as the atmosphere of a 'certain' child-rearing culture. For most of the time, adults demanded that children should behave well. To 'compensate' for this, children were allowed a great deal of freedom in their own activities, such as in playing outdoors.

Playgrounds in the 1950s were equipped with swings, and playground slides. Small carousels were put in motion when children kicked their feet, and offered a permissible dizziness to children in many parks and playgrounds.

In guides written for parents in the 1950s, such as the *Mother and Father's Book*, there were recommendations for what were acceptable levels of tolerance of chaos and disorder in dizzy play. On one double page of the book, it says, 'On the whole, 5–6-year-olds are able to plan their play acting peacefully . . . but sometimes they have to be able to fight a little' (Olsson 1956). 'Sometimes they have to be able to fight a little' does not encourage parents to favour fighting. Instead, it helps parents to understand both the polarized play acting we looked at in the chapters on make-believe play, and also encourages them to support dizzy play, and its disorderliness and chaos, as indispensable phenomena in life.

Dizzy play today

Throughout this book, we have seen how parents feel less certain in the ways of bringing up their children than they did in the 1950s.

This was explored fully in earlier chapters. It seems that less certain child-rearing practices create more space for dizzy play.

The 'uncertain' child-rearing culture of today has created a situation in which things are not as clear as they were in the 1950s. This means that adults have to evaluate each situation as it occurs, in order to decide how much and what kind of dizzy raging play is to be allowed. We need to bear in mind that general restlessness and lack of concentration are completely different from dizzy play.

Today we see:

- Children who turn the real world upside down. Emilia, Elisa and Niina would rush forward when the red light was on, and fall on a heap of corpses. A moment of irrational, raging dizziness is there. The girls changed the way real traffic lights behave, so that boundaries of real life vanished, and anarchy reigned.
- The wild play in the hall is another example of this. Mira, Juulia and Minttu unceasingly bombarded the boys who climbed on the side wall with tit-pimppi-pippeli taunts. The teasing of the girls' culminated in an adults' level of joke about Snow White which turned the fairy tale upside down and gave a new tone to the story of 'Snow White and the Seven Dwarfs'.

Dizzy play is not a new phenomenon, but it is different today from the 1950s.

Dizzy play is yet another aspect of play which depends on time and culture. What is experienced as dizzy, titillating or thrilling varies according to the historic period and culture. Dizzy play involving sexual references is nothing new. In Leea Virtanen's research from the 1960s to the 1970s, the topic of sex is presented as an aspect of children's play culture that is hidden from adult eyes. Brian Sutton-Smith and Diana Kelly-Byrne (1986) did report on sexual themes seen in the play-acting of 7-year-old girls and girls under school age, but the backgrounds of the girls in that study were thought to explain the sexual emphasis in their play, which was not seen as typical.

When Finnish children of today 'make love' at the day-care centre – a girl under a boy – it is as a consequence of general trends in child-rearing practices and the overt references and visibility of sex in the society of today, rather than an outcome of the backgrounds of some children.

In reality, it is difficult to gauge the changes that have taken place since the 1950s in relation to sex themes in the dizzy play of children for the following reasons:

- There are no reliably comparable research studies.

- Yet we know that children living in the 1950s without television operated in their play without so many of the explicit external images experienced today through television, advertisements and less 'certain' parenting. This means that children today more often than in the 1950s, see and hear things relating to sex before they can understand them. This shows clearly in the sexual themes they explore in their dizzy play.
- Dizzy play involving sexual themes is being experienced more often, and by younger and younger children.

In this chapter, we have seen that even dizzy play seems to change according to time and culture.

Questions for reflective practice

- Are you comfortable when children engage in dizzy play?
- How do you react?
- Will you change your thinking after reading this chapter? If so, why and how? If not, why?

Further reading

Isaacs, S. (1933) *Social Development in Young Children*. London: Routledge and Kegan Paul.
Sutton-Smith, B. (1972) Games of order and disorder. Paper presented at the Annual Meeting of the American Anthropological Association, Toronto, Canada. Reprinted in *The Dialectics of Play*, 1976. Schorndorf: Verlag Hoffman.

9

PLAY THAT DEFIES CATEGORIZATION

It is not possible to classify all play using the four categories (*agon, alea, mimicry* and *ilinx*) of Caillois. In Finland there are traditional kinds of play which defy this kind of classification.

Maija makes angels in the snow. She lies down and moves her arms so that the wings of the angel appear in the snow. At the same time she makes the skirt of the angel through moving her feet. When she stands up, she leaves behind her the impression of an angel.

Elisa draws with a felt pen a heart with an arrow piercing it on the arm of another girl and finishes her drawing with 'a puddle full of blood there under the drops'.

What the children are doing is, without doubt:

- voluntary
- detached from ordinary life
- unproductive.

So, the essential criteria for play are fulfilled. But the typical characteristics of play we are following in this book, which involve:

- the fascination of competition
- chance
- imitation
- dizziness

seem to be maladjusted in this play. For example, this kind of play is repeated and carried out 'according to the rules', but we search in vain for the least sign of competition.

Although angels in the snow and hearts with arrows piercing them 'imitate' children's own culture, there is:

- no role taking;
- no creating a shared illusion;
- no creating something new.

The naughty rhymes Mika and Tiina know are at one level dizzy, but there are many other rhymes which are funny but not naughty.

These examples keep the traditional rules of the heritage of folklore. Children learn them from older children and teach them to the next child generation. Although this kind of material was very scanty in the play acting of the 6-year-olds today, it has been the focus of many studies of children's lore.

Questions for reflective practice

- Using some of the techniques from Chapter 1, observe a child at play and interpret your observations to see if there is competition, chance and destiny, imitation and dizziness.
- Try to observe, analyse and interpret children's play from different perspectives. What is the meaning of play for the child? How involved are they in their play?
- How can you support children as they develop their play? What is your role as a practitioner?

Further reading

Opie, I. and Opie, P. (1970) *Children's Games in Street and Playground.* Oxford: Oxford University Press.

10

GENDER AND CHILDREN'S PLAY CULTURE

In the play culture of children we can easily identify three parts which only partly overlap each other:

- boys' play culture;
- girls' play culture;
- a shared area of boys' and girls' play culture.

Boys' play culture

Children who live in the same culture have a shared understanding of many matters. By the age of 6, children are able to collect potential material and ideas which can be used in their play. However, there is variation in what children find interesting and 'store' for further use in play.

Girls and boys partly share the world of play, but they also have their own interests when they play. As Riikka puts it: 'Well, sometimes they play differently ... sometimes play together and sometimes separately and sometimes somewhat mixed ... so I don't really know.' Riku puts the way girls and boys play very simply: 'They play differently and different games and in a different way.'

Juuso: They play different games and we play different games.
MK: What do they play?
Juuso: I don't know.
MK: Do you play something together?
Juuso: Nooo [a long no]
MK: Nothing.

Juuso: Yes, always when the girls come we leave.
MK: You don't care about girls' play very much.
Juuso: No, nobody does.
MK: Someone talked about playing kiss tag.
Juuso: But we don't play it, because we are so fast we throw them off the scent.
MK: You throw them off the scent.
Juuso: I am the quickest in the day-care centre, so they can't catch me and not Mika or Jonas either, because they are also so quick.

In his speech Juuso constructs an image of a separate world of play for boys. From his point of view, girls' play acting is so unimportant that boys do not even want to know about it. Sometimes girls try to approach boys with their stupid issues but because boys are so incomparable due to their quickness they leave girls far behind them and go to their own games. Juuso also makes it very clear that he is not just talking about himself but also the other boys in the group. Saying 'nobody does' gives more weight to what he says. It changes his personal view into a universally applicable fact.

If we take a closer look at what Juuso says, it is easy to find that his construction of boys' play neither corresponds to the reality described by other children nor to my observations. Instead he sketches the ideal image of reality that he wants to give to other people. Of all the boys, Juuso is the one who most consistently constructs his masculine ideal. He is the leader in football. He fights against the evil ones as a Power Ranger or a Biker Mouse. He directs fights when playing with his Lego constructions at home. He is the quickest runner at the day-care centre. He distances himself from the girls, and he demonstrates his own status in the hierarchy of the group of boys with whom he plays.

However, when he is at home each evening, Juuso gives up his 'male' role. 'Here are all my bedtime toys' he says, presenting three soft well-worn Steiner dolls. Beside them there is a soft fish in the corner of his bed: 'Oh, that fish, it is my bedtime fish if the other toys get lost.'

Girls' play culture

Tiia and Anu try to crystallize the essential nature of girls' play acting in a few sentences:

Tiia: Well, girls like to play with Barbies and My Little Ponies and . . .

Anu: Boys think they are disgusting!
Tiia: Yes, and then boys play wars and that kind of thing and all
         kinds of war . . .
Anu: Yes, and then girls mostly play something beautiful . . .
Tiia: Yes, and peaceful . . .
(A short pause)
Anu: More beautiful and peaceful.
Tiia: Yes, boys play all kinds of violent games and girls don't play
         very violent games.

As they describe this beautiful and peaceful world, the girls stop, enchanted by their ideal world of girls' play they have created. In the same way as Juuso created an idealized world of boys' play, Tiia and Anu simplify their ideal into a dream of a beautiful and peaceful world of play for girls.

Having done this, they return to a more realistic state. The 'absolutely' beautiful and peaceful is softened to become simply 'more beautiful and peaceful'. Then, when they say that 'boys play all kinds of violent games and girls do not play very violent games' the description is made even more real to them.

Juuso, Tiia and Anu seem to be aware that they are talking of idealized and unreal worlds of pure boys' play, full of violence or girls' play that is peaceful and beautiful, but they give clear signals that they want to play as girls and as boys in a way that is traditional for their gender.

The differences between the play of boys and girls depend on the kind of play. Overall, the differences in competition play, and games with rules, games of chance and destiny, or dizzy play do not show such marked differences as we see in make-believe and imitation play.

Gender and different games

Gender and street play and games with rules

Street play like church rat, tag and hide-and-seek and other games with rules which we have looked at earlier in the book are the kind of games that girls and boys play together. The rules are the same for everybody, and because everybody has to follow them, they eliminate segregation, including that based on gender. However, strategies for participation may vary from competing to 'playing with others'. Thus, it is possible that compared with girls, many boys have a more competitive attitude in this kind of play because they evaluate their hierarchical position in the group also in many other situations. So, in the attitude towards this kind of play, there is room for both individual and gender-based variation although there is nothing in the structure of these games that would force or even persuade boys and girls to take a different stand towards this kind of play (Bjerrum-Nielsen and Rudberg 1991; Harris 1998).

The only exception is kiss tag play, where the roles are gender-based. Girls chase the boys. In this game the girls maintain the tension between boys and girls, whereas boys are more passive.

Riku: Girls try to kiss.
MK: They really kiss you?
Joni: Yes, yes, they do.
MK: Is it nice?
Riku: Yes, when they catch you they try to kiss you, nothing else.
MK: Do you try to kiss them sometimes?
Riku: Never. Not ever.

Riku is the only boy who admits that being kissed by a girl could be fun. But it is obvious that the game would quickly fade if the boys just found it annoying. However, it is important for the boys to feel that they are filling the role expectations of boys, and that they never kiss the girls.

Games of luck, chance and destiny

Play based on luck, chance and destiny is also shared between boys and girls. Of course, to be the one who 'counts' may mean more to one child than another but good or bad luck hits anyone, regardless of their skill. It is worth mentioning that girls, more often than boys, let destiny resolve casting in their play because roles in girls' play-acting are seldom as hierarchical as that of boys.

Gender and dizzy play

Both boys and girls are interested in dizzy play. Sometimes this kind of play bursts out without asking for permission. Sometimes players consciously seek out physical dizziness, or the dizziness that comes from turning the world upside down conceptually, but gender does not seem to be an essential factor in either of the situations.

Gender and the world of make-believe

In this kind of play, gender is a meaningful factor. Children like Antti, Anu, Emmi, Kalle, Mika, Noora, Juuso and Tiia talk as if Barbies and soldiers symbolize the extremities of masculinity and femininity. These toy figures represent the contrasting arenas of human relationships and fighting The more play acting is about fighting and war, the more unlikely it is that girls will join the play – especially in the roles of fighters, even though these are crucial in the game. On the other hand, the more human relationships and feelings are the focus of the play, the less likely boys are to participate in the central roles.

What the children say about gender and play ■

The way the children talk about their play strengthens the differences between boys and girls.

Boys

Emmi: Boys play with soldiers and girls don't like them.
Sanna: Well, only boys pretend they are Power Rangers.
Noora: Boys don't want to play with Barbies, they find it like talking rubbish.
Kalle: We just don't play with Barbies, that's the only thing.

Girls

Mika: Girls play in the sand box and boys make war play.
Antti: Girls don't care about Power Rangers.

Fighting games are boys' games also in the sense that they are organized by boys even when girls participate in them. Boys also occupy the most important roles whereas girls are given – or they actively choose – meaningless minor roles. Similarly, girls direct playing house and give the boys the roles that do not focus on feelings.

In adventure play, the situation is different. This kind of play has the structure of a story. From the beginning, the players are able to solve problems and reach a happy end. In both their own stories and those inspired by television, there are numerous human and animal adventurers and adventuresses. Thus there are enough inviting roles for boys and girls.

The gender differences in play are meaningful

The fact that boys and girls participate in different kinds of games and that they participate differently in the same kind of games reflects the gender-based world of both children and adults. Boys and girls fill their potential storage for play only partly with the same material. The differences are meaningful. Girls sieve out the 'human relationship material' from what they experience, hear and see, unlike boys who are interested in all forms of 'action'.

Toys and gender

It is possible to follow the differences in orientation from the micro-level of toys and toy brochures to wider adaptation of influences of the adult world. Adult producers of children's culture bring the gendered world of toys within reach of children through toy brochures. Six-year-olds read them like experts. Emmi complains: 'There [in the toy brochure that came yesterday] were an awful lot of toys for boys . . .'. Maria is satisfied: 'Yes, but there were all kinds of nice things for girls at the beginning, a kind of toy world.'

Even Lego™ no longer believes in gender-neutral blocks. Instead, Lego™ tells ready-made stories for girls and boys: cosy Belleville stories for girls and exciting pirate or space stories for boys. Antti, Emmi, Katariina and Tiia are typical in knowing the classification in three categories: toys for babies, girls and boys.

However, Kalle and Mikael avoid stereotypes. They do not immediately reject everything aimed for girls: 'Well, I [admit that I] like Tiia's Barbie car.' 'I like the beach issue [Polly Pocket miniature scene], but nothing else, all the rest are quite stupid.' However, boys take from girls' issues toys that fit boys best: a car and 'pollari' [Polly Pocket] with a boat and three or four guys.

Television programmes and gender

Television programmes are also divided into three by children but the division is somewhat different. There are programmes for girls, boys and for both.

MK: Do you find that girls and boys watch different programmes?
Riku: Yes, for example, girls watch *Pikku kakkonen* [Little two, children's television].
MK: You don't watch it?

Riku: No, it sickens me, I don't like it any more.
MK: Why?
Riku: There are always such childish issues . . . (laughing) such child-
        ish issues happen that I can't even watch it.
Joni: I never watch it, never ever.

Juuso, Riku and Joni talk about a stereotype who is a 'hard guy'
who contrasts with soft and childish girls. Boys find that the kind of
childish issues that they have already left behind still fit 'women'.

Boys like *Power Rangers, Biker Mice*, and *Jurassic Park*. Some of the
boys find that not even *Biker Mice* are equal to *Power Rangers* 'because
there are not such hard issues and good issues in them'. *Power Rangers*
issues are so hard that in spite of all exhalation boys have to admit
that 'they were rather frightening' (Mikael).

The move from children's 'thrillers' to adult thrillers means more
and more thrilling and frightening experiences for children. 'I have
seen too exciting movies', Mikael admits. Antti has seen 'police series,
terribly frightening films'. Mikke and Kalle are of the same mind that
Terminator is the most horrifying programme they have ever seen.
Jesse's parents explain that he has been trained to watch programmes
based on violence with his parents by saying that blood is nothing but
ketchup.

Boys need mental pictures of heroism, autonomy, fighting between
good and evil, power and the use of power when constructing their
identity. They collect impressions and motives of these themes from
real life and from stories told by television, videos and movies. What
happens though is that boys not only receive what they are looking
for but also an overdose of excitement and violence that they find too
exciting and frightening. Some 77 per cent of Finnish 5–6-year-old
children say that television programmes are frightening (Lahikainen
and Kraav 1996).

Girls' interest in human relationships leads to a different kind of
situation but their world does not, as Juuso suggests, consist only of
home sphere and children's television. Sanna says: 'I watch *Pikku
kakkonen* but it's rather childish.' Girls like to watch *Dalmatians* and
Lion King. They like stories that enable them to experience the whole
range of feelings through one of the role figures. Anu, Emmi, Maija,
Maria, Minna, Noora and Riikka all enjoy these kinds of programmes.
Naturally the plot is equally interesting in these stories and also many
boys like to watch them. Sanna also knows *Hilarius the mouse* produced by the 'Centre for Education of the Church'. *Power Rangers* are
not interesting but Emmi, Noora and Susanna, watch *Biker Mice*.

With their mothers, many of the girls like Anu, Emmi, Maria and
Sofia watch soap series where human relationships are tackled from

one part to another without ever getting to 'the End', like *Bold and Beautiful, The Blonde Came to the House* and *Kotikatu* (Home Street).

Kotikatu represents Finish television realism. Kotikatu is a family series in which the course of events are credible. Sex is presented 'nicely'. There is seldom violence and the use of it is problematized. Drunken people are shown but there is no wallowing in drinking. Within the demand of 'nice contents' themes like mental illness, pair relationship problems, problems with alcohol and unemployment have been tackled.

The producers of the series might find the tameness of the series as a limitation in their work (*Helsingin Sanomat*, 28 September 1997 and 11 April 1999) but from the perspective of 6-year-olds this is not a problem. Children find the complex world of adults unstable. When many children are afraid of their parents' quarrels and divorce and the greater part of 5–6-year-olds mention that television programmes make them afraid, it is probable that even family television series arouse fear and embarrassment in some children just because they are so realistic (Lahikainen 1997)

What is unambiguously 'too much' for girls is plain sex, that is too intimate for some of the 6-year-olds. Breasts, making love and oral sex make Juulia cover her eyes with her hands but at the same time she is curious and the desire to peep through her fingers and listen time after time to the same shivering stories about oral sex is strong.

The image that I have sketched of the separated worlds of boys and girls is of course simplified. Although girls have competitions about who has the longest hair, Riikka and Tiina say that they sometimes also go to the hall of the day-care centre in order to train in karate kicks. Some of the girls are more boyish than others. Tiina is a tomboy and she plays more than most with boys, especially with Kalle and Mikke. Although Mika says that 'swearing, spitting and speaking kind of dirty issues in the swing' is typical for boys, even a boyish boy like Juuso may be a puppy or a kitten in adventure play or take care of soft dolls. Petri still plays in the home corner with the girls with whom Antti used to play when he was small.

Nevertheless, it is easy to tell the exceptions to the rule. Tiina, Miia, Antti, Juuso and Tuomas operate with concepts like 'mostly' and 'sometimes'. What is interesting though is that children usually refer to exceptions in a neutral way without admiration or disregard. However, it seems to be more uncomplicated for a girl to move towards more 'rough issues' than for a boy to move towards more 'beautiful issues'. A boy has to be careful in order to avoid getting too girlish whereas a girl can extend her territory towards boys' territory. Thus, there is no need to worry if a girl is e.g. interested in football.

Margaretha Rönnberg (1997) divides boys' and girls' world of play into two by listing figures boys and girls identify themselves with. According to her, girls are fascinated by beauty, a bride, a mother, an independent career woman, a bitch, a witch, a nice girl and a stupid blonde whereas boys are fascinated by a lone wolf, a policeman, a sheriff, a superhero, a saviour, a friend, a helper, a joke teller and a secret agent. Although all of these roles are not to be found in the material of this research, the list by Rönnberg is indicative by its 'boys will be boys, girls will be girls' spirit.

It may be concluded that children do not find that they choose gender-based play acting in order to fulfil the role expectations of adults or children. Instead, when children choose for themselves, the voluntariness of play spontaneously generates the play acting of boys and girls.

Questions for reflective practice

• Have you noticed signs of a play culture developed by boys?
• Have you found evidence in your observations of a play culture of girls?
• Do you agree that there are shared areas of boys' and girls' play culture?

Further reading

Bruce, T. (1996) *Helping Young Children to Play*. London: Hodder and Stoughton.
Gussin Paley, V. (1984) *Boys* and *Girls: Superheroes in the Doll Corner*. Chicago: University of Chicago Press.
Holland, P. (2003) *We Don't Play with Guns Here: War, Weapons and Superhero Play in the Early Years*. Maidenhead: Open University Press.

11

ADULTS AND PLAY

Adults create the framework for play

Adults inevitably influence children's own play culture, even though they might seem to be in the background. We need to look at how adults have both a direct and an indirect impact on children's play.

Adults create the framework for play. This defines:

- what children experience;
- the way that time is regulated for giving children opportunities to play;
- the way that physical space for play is made available;
- the materials provided for play.

Adult conceptions of play are of special interest. Because adult attitudes to play are not detached from other phenomena, they need to be linked to the dominating child-rearing culture as well. We need to see how the changing roles of both parents and professionals are reflected in their attitudes to the children's play.

Uncertain parents

Antti's father explains his approach. He says that he tries to let his son have his own way as far as possible and so he listens to him:

I find that you have to listen to the child as much as possible.

or

I usually let him decide or I make alternative suggestions.

But Emilia's father wonders about this:

> When you take your children to the day-care centre, it is very unclear for many parents which are the issues parents decide and which are the issues children can decide . . . It is curious. Children make decisions about strange things. Often you see parents coax children to do something, with long talks – everyday issues like should we go in for lunch, do you take your raincoat . . . trivial issues, There are negotiations about these and more. Parents try to make children say what they want them to say . . . It is just about avoiding conflicts.

Although Antti's father talks as an insider and Emilia's father as an outsider, the uncertain child-rearing practices show in the way that both of them talk.

Mikael's mother agrees with Emmi's mother that everything can be negotiated. Jukka's mother describes life with children as free and unrestrained.

After five years in Finland Jonas's Lithuanian parents describe how they see a typical Finnish upbringing:

Jonas's father: You should watch *The Moomins* on television. It is just like real life . . . children are allowed to do their own things.

Jonas's mother: And at the day-care centres they educate an individual, a person. They understand the child, not just as part of the whole group.

Yet Jonas's mother also sees the reverse side:

> I don't know about day-care centres but in the street or in the bus . . . sometimes children behave too freely, we never let them be so free, we want them to be more polite, sometimes I see that children are allowed to do whatever they want to . . . they can sit on another person if they want.

Jonas' parents know both the strengths and weaknesses of the Finnish child-rearing culture. The comparisons with Moomins stories, and a child who sits on other people on the bus, describe how the emphasis on individual freedom can at its extreme, turn against itself.

Minna's mother seeks the balance that Jonas's parents suggest has been lost sometimes. She describes her ideal as a compromise that combines the best parts of the educational experiments of the past decades. She admits with a sigh that it is not easy to follow one's principles. Many boundaries slip and slide and change and not even a conscious striving for authoritative education is enough when there is no united conception of education.

The boundary between adulthood and childhood can quickly become obscure. Jukka's mother says, 'I love to be like this, I am still childlike myself . . . I think that I will never grow that way . . . like with Milla [9 years] we are good friends, she can tell me anything, I am like her girl friend. I don't want to be just her mother.'

Single parents in particular find signs of pal parents in themselves. 'When we are just the two of us, . . . we don't have adults' and children's issues' (Maria's mother). Emmi's mother shares this but goes on to say: '. . . but somehow I still want to keep the role of parents in that parents have still lived a bit longer, and they have experience of many issues.'

The mothers of Jukka, Maria and Emmi all describe different forms of pal parenthood:

- Jukka's mother wants to be a friend to her daughter.
- Maria's mother does not maintain the difference between adults' and children's affairs.
- Emmi's mother states that she is a pal mother in many senses. However, she does not try to reach full pal parenthood. Instead she wants to maintain her adult role in certain situations.

Hobbies

It is through their children's hobbies that parents try to consciously educate their children. Children start their hobbies strikingly earlier than in the 1950s. A 6-year-old nowadays might have three hobbies weekly after a full day at the day-care centre (i.e. 40 hours a week).

The mothers of Emmi, Maria and Niina appreciate the abundance of alternative hobbies. In their childhood, there were very few possibilities for hobbies in an ordinary family. However, Niina's mother asks whether children under seven years of age really want 'all kinds of music groups and dance lessons'. Finding the right balance among all these rich offerings is her problem.

Computers are often introduced into the family home. 'The earlier the better', Kalle's mother says, 'Computers are the future. It is quite crazy to forbid them from children. It makes no sense. On the contrary, they learn incredibly easily to cope with it.' If children want to learn about computers, then without doubt, they learn incredibly easily how to work it. The same applies to hobbies. If children have an inner motivation, they love to learn ballet, play the piano or ice-hockey as a pleasure. But what about a child who does not want to have any hobbies?

Maija's father: We have consciously avoided going to certain clubs and other places, so we have not started any training at all, the most important reason is that we do not have the energy.

Maija's mother: I have tried with Maija . . . but she has definitely said that day-care is her hobby and that she wants to be at home and I have found that much better. A lot of 6-year-olds already have a lot of hobbies, and once in a while I have to confess that as an ambitious mother I find myself thinking that Maija should do this or that.

Maija's father: Me too, I find myself thinking that she could start to study foreign languages.

Maija's mother: But on the other hand she always seems to have something to do at home. She does so many things quite independently, and then one asks again why we should feel we have to organize something special. We are at home together, and everybody has something to do and the atmosphere is peaceful and cosy . . . Children are trained from early age.

We later find Emmi building blocks of houses on the kitchen floor together with her father which seems to be time well spent, albeit without any set timetable.

Emmi's parents don't want to hurry her. Now Emmi uses her language skills in her zoo play that spreads from her bedroom into the hall. She writes signs with animals' names and places them on their cages. Emmi has both time and space for her playing.

The staff – supporters of play at the day-care centre

The importance of play is so self-evidently a part of the Finnish day-care culture that it is unnecessary to give reasons for it: 'Naturally, it is the most important activity.' In Finland the Froebelian tradition with its strong emphasis on play lies behind this unquestioned status of play.

Kindergarten teachers and nursery nurses find that play is a central and natural thing in children's lives. The voluntary nature of play enhances learning. Children do not play in order to learn but learning comes as a by-product when children are spontaneously motivated. The staff members of the day-care centres are 'on the side of play'. At least, this appears so in the way that they talk about play.

However, it seems that a general understanding of play, which staff can describe vividly and with conviction, does not match the practice. In one group discussion the practitioners talked about a piece of plastic tarpaulin that had probably appeared on the playground from the nearby market place. Elina says, 'The best toy was a terrible plastic cover that had come from the market place.' Arja continues, 'It was good for building huts.' Riitta ends the discussion, 'But it was always so dusty and muddy that it disappeared last week.'

The 'terrible cover' is identified as 'the best toy' and tolerated as such for some time. But then the earlier situation, without covers, returns, in spite of the sustained success of the cover.

The statement that, 'play is the most important issue' means that the practitoners recognize and enjoy intensive play. But why didn't the adults get more tarpaulins when they saw how much one single one stimulated the children's play? Why did they not at least get a new one instead of the dusty and muddy one? Why do the children not ask for more tarpaulins so that they can make better huts?

In the day-care culture there are plenty of unspoken rules that everybody follows. The adults do not have to say: 'We are not people to ask for materials for your play.' Children know that without the need to say anything. They have never heard an adult say: 'Whenever you need something for your play, just let me know and we will see what we can do.'

At the same day-care centre children tell me that it is 'messy' to build huts, which indicates that they have adopted the attitudes of the adults at the day care centre.

Adult engagement in children's play

Practitioner attitudes to play have to be examined in several ways in order to see how a general appreciation of play is realized in practice. How much autonomy do adults give to children's play? How sensitive are the adults in relation to play? How do adults stimulate children's play? Autonomy, sensitivity and stimulation are concepts that have been used, e.g. for evaluation of the teacher style in research on the quality of early childhood education (Lecuers 1994; Pascal and Bertram 1995). Here the concepts are used to clarify the different dimensions of the adult role.

Ulla tells us about some boys who were indulging in rough play:

It was only running and fists and kind of fighting. I thought if I
let it go on . . . These boys are new to each other so I didn't know
how much they would tolerate it when the other one swipes
with his fist, even though he doesn't hit. But it could have
become rather rough and someone might get hurt and start a
battle for real, so we changed . . . and the boys then said that
they want some fighting game so I asked what about wrestling,
so OK, if you let us wrestle we'll do that and so we made a
wrestling game and boys were satisfied . . . perhaps we'll play
Power Rangers, too, when I know them better, and know that
the game is safe.

Ulla cannot ignore the play, which is fighting, unruly, aggressive and
noisy. She sets the boundary: you are allowed to play at wrestling, but
not to fight, hurt or injure the others. These are common principles in
early years' settings. Adults intervene in the play, but only when
necessary, i.e. when fighting exceeds the tolerance of adults or a conflict becomes real.

The striving for maximum freedom of children's own play is also
seen positively in many ways. The play ground of Ulpukka day-care
centre is small. In order to enhance children's possibilities for
undisturbed play the practitioners have agreed with the children that
they are allowed to play outside the fence near the playground.

The 'stretching' of boundaries is also seen in the attitudes of the
practitioners towards toys. Now My Little Pony, Barbie, Power
Rangers and Biker Mice can enter early years' settings. In the 1950s,
Donald Duck was out of question in the playing houses area. Yet the
increasingly permissive attitude does not, the staff of Kesäkumpu suggest, indicate adults' interest or appreciation of this kind of toy. In
Riitta's view, it simply reflects children's 'wants'.

It is easy for the adults not to watch the television programmes or
films to which the toys are linked, but the characters wander into the
day-care centre as toys. Children want to bring toys, and adults do not
want to forbid this.

However, there are some toys that evoke discussion among the
staff: Barbie dolls for girls and guns and swords for boys.

Barbies have always made adults feel ill at ease. When the first Barbie
was created in 1959, her breasts evoked disbelief and opposition
among toy manufacturers: the designer had to fight for her high bust
idea against men who defended asexual dolls.

At the day-care centre, the excuse for Barbie is that 'There is still the
family in their play.' It is just that Barbie dolls look different. This
interpretation of 'Barbie play' solves the contradiction that easily
takes place in the adult's mind. An adult intuitively reads the codes of

the superficial feminine and sexy Barbie and feels uncomfortable. It helps to think that playing with Barbie dolls is still what it used to be – independent of Barbie's bust measurement.

At the day-care centres Barbie demonstrates the permissive attitudes of adults. But the head of Ulpukka day-care centre never buys Barbies: 'The small budget has to be used in another way, more pedagogically.' If children give old Barbies to the day-care centre they are welcome, because they add to the Barbies girls bring to the day-care centre any way. The day-care centre Hilapieli is more liberal. Girls are allowed to bring their own Barbies to the day-care centre and also the centre budget is used to buy them.

Boys, guns and swords – boys will be boys

The changing attitudes to weapons and war games indicate how far adults accept boys' games. All the practitioners comment on how the prohibition against weapons and wars was abandoned in most of the day-care centres in the early 1990s. The change in attitudes was fast. Still in the 1980s, war games were forbidden as opposing peace education. When 4-year-old Janne saw an adult, he quickly turned his self-made wooden sword upside down and said with a honeyed smile: 'Look, I made a Jesus Christ cross!' This unforgettable example comes from the day-care centre of Marttila at the beginning of the 1970s. It illustrates the difficulty of peace education through forbidding war games. Instead of supporting an internalized attitude, adults easily strengthen hypocrisy (see Holland 2003).

Today, these 'good old days of peace' are reminisced about with amusement. It is a relief for the staff that weapon play is now allowed, because the children engage in pretend shooting any way. Elina, Sinikka and Raila recall how 'boys made guns by gnawing them out of the rye crisps'. In Kesäkumpu children are now allowed to prepare weapons out of wood or of different kinds of construction sets such as Lego™. If war play is restricted, it is not because of the play idea as such but because of the noise.

Helena says: 'We have received war toys as gifts from our "old children", a surprisingly large number of them, so that we have e.g. soldiers and tanks with which they play. They are now toys belonging to the day-care centre, and boys have wonderful games with them.'

There are many kinds of war play: fighting with swords or guns as well as constructing frontiers and shelters for plastic soldiers. Building the scene for war is sometimes the main activity that players are involved in for a long time. The more war play approaches construction play, the less ambivalent are the adults about it. In the same way as adults are reassured by the connection of Barbie to playing houses, the meaning of war play and war toys is tamed by connecting them to organized constructing.

The dominant attitude is that adults do not interfere in the children's play. Children are, both at the same time, allowed and forced to build their play all by themselves.

Yet, do the adults know what the children play? It is hard to mark off the boundary between positive and negative autonomy in children's play. There is a permanent tension between respect for children's intimacy and secrets, on the one hand, and control and enrichment of children's activities, on the other. Children need both sensitive supervision and stimulation and freedom when they develop their inner self, not either/or but both/and (Van Maanen and Lavering 1996).

How do adults know when they ought to interfere in children's play and when not? Here are three principles which help us to tease out the adult role in children's play:

1 Sensitivity to play
2 Informed observation of play
3 Knowing the world of children

The first principle, the sensitivity to perceive what playing means for children is closely connected to the ability to observe. Educators, who do not really 'see' the child, cannot fully bear their pedagogical responsibility.

The importance of the second principle has been emphasized throughout the history of kindergarten teacher training. In Finnish early childhood education 'Sei außerlich passiv und innerlich aktiv' (be externally passive and internally active) was one of the vital Froebelian slogans that directs the conscious observation of children. It was important to adapt this slogan especially during free play. The adult did not actively participate in play, but instead observed consciously what the playing was like.

The erosion of this principle can be seen in the playgrounds of the day-care centres. We see adults chatting together on the edges. Adults are at a distance from children, and consequently the observation of play is more often superficial and general than deep and detailed. The oldest children easily move out of the sight or at least out of the understanding of adults.

As for the third principle, in order to understand what play is about, it is also necessary to know the children's world. The 'wrestling play' example we looked at earlier in the chapter also illustrates the separate worlds of adults and children. Eija says, 'I am too tired to watch children's programmes on TV in the evening.' This comment shows the dominant attitude towards children's popular culture and the play that is based on it.

Riitta finds that watching children's programmes is important (but only in theory, it seems, and not in practice): 'I should watch *Biker Mice* and others in order to know a little about them but I never have time.' It is evident that practitioners can reveal their ignorance without shame.

Elina is the exception: 'I find we have to know these Modos and Vinnies and Throttles so that we are able to support children when they are playing, like asking them what happened next etc. . . . but the children are clever and they can tell if the teacher really knows or if she is pretending to know.'

Grasping the basic idea of the series only demands about half an hour per programme. Staff might together watch and discuss programmes influencing the children's play. The practitioners appreciate play on a general level, but do not see the need to understand what it means for the children in practice. This needs reflection on the part of all practitioners.

Because adults in Finnish early years settings try to avoid a definitive 'no' to play involving some toys, or themes, a compromising attitude is taken, along the lines of, 'Well, let them play.' This is in the spirit of a generally permissive child-rearing culture. Barbies, Turtles, Biker Mice and Power Rangers are accepted, but they are placed in a category in which adults do not have to know or appreciate anything about them, even though they may be extremely important to the children. Naturally, knowing the children's issues is not enough to become a sensitive adult but sharing the children's cultural competence offers a good starting point for understanding the children's play. Nor does this mean an uncritical approach to commercial television programmes or supplementary products.

How practitioners can enrich children's play

In the curriculum of the Hilapieli day-care centre, staff have indicated that children are at the point in their development where they enjoy 'games with rules', showing that Piaget's stages of play are known by these practitioners. Reaching the 'period of games with rules' means that children are interested in games with rules and are able to play them. Yet knowing this does not seem to encourage the practitioners to teach games with rules to children to encourage the children to play these games independently.

Niina's mother says:

> I have had children here at different times for almost ten years. I have seen their practice, and I really wonder why they have so seldom had traditional games with rules. It is less than ten times that I have seen these kinds of game . . . of course I understand free play but one would think that in all these years there would have been more of these games, because they are really nice, and 6-year-olds are already able to play these games very well . . . traditional games, a little more. I don't know but I think that it is their right [to teach games with rules] but they don't take it up.

The passive role of adults outdoors probably explains their passivity in relation to games with rules as well.

In Ulpukka, they sometimes have gym outdoors and then they have traditional games, especially in the spring. But this day-care centre is an exception.

Arja feels that adults ought to intervene if children cannot get involved in play. At the same time she is unclear how the adult should help the children to 'start to construct the playing'.

> It is common to see a child wander from one place to another. They cannot begin to play . . . we need to support the long-lasting play . . . we could ask them to choose what to play. The child can choose as they do in free play, but it means that the child can't move from play to play.

In the autumn of 1994 the children of Kesäkumpu day-care centre repeatedly played the dramatic shipwreck of the *Estonia*. This kind of play acting evokes controversial emotions, but television news cannot be ignored. Arja says:

> These news items come through the media and from everywhere . . . you cannot avoid them, . . . they should be adapted somehow in children's play acting so that we really teach children how to use them in play, but you have to reflect on what would be the best way.

Arja is trying to find an answer to the question, what should adults do when children's play ideas evoke anxiety in adults? She hesitates between an active and passive role.

'Wandering children' and 'children who tackle news in their playing' are not new phenomena. The same challenges repeat year after year, but the definition of the adult's role remains unresolved by the practitioners.

The challenge of encouraging wandering children to participate in sustained play does not become any easier if it is placed in the wider context of uncertain child-rearing practices and the 'interruption culture' that is typical of the postmodern way of living. There is accumulating evidence of the 'interruption culture' in the day-care centres gathered through my own observations and the feedback of the kindergarten teacher students.

According to Harriet Strandell, 'Children are enormously flexible and they are able to change their plans consistently. Children have internalized well the way of living of today because we all live in the same way' (*Lastentarha* 1/1995).

Juha Siltala's (1997) interpretation of the connection between children's day-care centre life and adults' way of living is different. When adults get used to continual interruptions, they begin to demand the same of children. Naturally there are differences between day-care centres. Henri's mother says, 'In Ulpukka, often when I go there children are playing peacefully in their small corners.'

When we try to understand the 'wandering children' we also have to focus on their past. The 6-year-olds have already played for many years. There are many factors that explain why children become or do not become involved in their play. One of these is the personal 'play history' of everybody:

- Did adults support children's make-believe play when the first signs of it emerged?
- Did adults strengthen the vague inner images by participating in make-believe play?

According to research by Pirkko Mäntynen (1997), the support for make-believe play of under-three-year-olds is insufficient at most of the day-care centres. There is too little direct and indirect support of play. There are too few toys and other play materials and the group is divided too rarely and the rhythm of the day is inadequate. The 6-year-olds who are only half-involved in their play may well have many years of 'wandering' behind them, which is then reflected in their inability to become engaged in sustained play at an age when 'they should already be able to play'.

The same kind of vaguely positive but passive attitude towards play has dominated in other Nordic countries also. Birgitta Knutdotter Olofsson summarizes the reasons for 'non playing', suggesting that adults do not show children that they appreciate play and they do not stimulate it. Adults hope that children will become involved in long-lasting play without disturbing others, but if this is not the case, adults are helpless.

However, as a counter-reaction to this, some researchers and ped-agogues have developed an active play pedagogic from very different perspectives. In Finland, e.g. Aili Helenius, in Sweden, Gunilla Lindqvist and Birgitta Knutsdotter Olofsson, in Norway, Kari Mjaaland Heggstadd, Ida M. Knudsen, Arne Trageton and Eli Åm, and in Denmark, Stig Broström and Torben Rasmussen have tried to enhance children's possibilities to play at the day-care centres. In England, Tina Bruce (1991, 1996, 2001, 2004) has tried to strengthen the role of make-believe play as a part of early childhood education in Key Stage 1, which tends to be oriented towards early learning through academic skills.

Parents and how they can support the children's play ∎

Playing at home

How do parents see the play of their children? In contrast to the wandering and unruliness reported by practitioners and observed by researchers in the day-care centres, parents describe the play at home as long-lasting and intensive. Riikka's mother, Noora's parents, Maija's parents, Juuso's mother, Emmi's mother, Sanna's mother all give the same message. Mikael's mother says, 'He plays for hours, it is the same game all the time . . . sometimes it's difficult to get him to eat.'

Parents find playing as the central or 'basic' activity during the years before school start. Many children like to play alone, but there are those who would like to play with a friend. Many parents are happy to invite a play pal home. Maria's mother says, 'It is a relief for me when Tomppa comes and plays with Maria. His mother always worries that I might find it tiring, but it is so much easier when they play together.'

In these situations, children need adults to 'transport' their play pals.

Parents supporting play by joining in with their children

What, how and why do parents play? Many mothers find make-believe play difficult. Riikka's mother says, 'I can't, I'm not childish in the way, I'm not a child, I'm an adult and I have a limited imagin-ation.' Niina's mother, anticipating fantasy playing with toys says, 'I would probably chat like an idiot with them.'

Minna's mother does not value her play skills highly either:

I play terribly badly. I start to yawn immediately. I always say five minutes. I don't mind playing those games. It is mostly nonsense, that now this one goes and hides, now this one is seeking, and I also find it a little irritating that the rules change all the time, I'm a rational adult . . . I feel that it drives me crazy if I have to play like this.

Emmi's, Maija's, Minna's and Niina's mothers find that the adult imagination does not stretch to this kind of play, and repeating the lines children give to adults is not satisfying either. Emilia's mother finds that it is much more rewarding to do something else together with her children.

Fathers disturb this basic model. Mika and Tiina's father finds that he is a good player because he participates fully. The architect father of Maija builds cities on the kitchen floor. 'We have built houses and blocks of flats and backyards and all that and then the cars come and fill all the places.' On the other hand, he says that he 'simply does not want to play any games'.

Emmi's, Joni's, Maija's and Minna's mothers, who avoid make-believe play, do enjoy playing games with their children. The unchangeable rules of games of competition in play help parents and their children to construct a shared framework. In addition, adults have defined many of the rules.

According to David Cohen (1993), fathers play more with their children than mothers do. The quality of fathers' and mothers' playing is also different.

Fathers' playing is both multifaceted and less intellectual than that of mothers. Children seem to enjoy playing with their fathers, probably because of the physical and social dimension of it (Cohen 1993). Dizzy play brings out the playfulness of fathers. The dizziness doesn't last long, but is nevertheless important. Adults may initiate dizzy play as much as children. Maija's father says:

Often it is tickling or fooling about or something like that. Sometimes we play on words or some ideas, so that one says something the wrong way round, or teases . . . I find that it is more that you feel that you are playing with your child and you do what you are not too tired to do after work.

Parents supporting the child's need for a close relationship with nature through their play

A close relationship to nature belongs to a good childhood. Most of the parents spontaneously talked about this. Parents deeply appreci-ate the days and weeks in their summer cottages. In Finland it is usual and considered important to go to the forest and be beside a lake. Sanna's mother, Antti's father, Tiia's mother, Mikael's mother, Riikka's mother, and Niina's mother all want to give this experience to their children. Emilia's mother summarizes the importance of moving and playing in the countryside, 'These are spinal cord issues. I am edu-cated in this way myself.'

Children who spend a great deal of time outdoors do not need their commercially manufactured toys or video games. Children have so much more freedom than in the city that it changes the way they play in remarkable ways. The examples Riikka's mother, Antti's father, Joni's father, Mika's father and Mikael's mother give are of water play, building huts and totems, or hunting wolves and foxes.

In the countryside, children have secret places and they can move almost as freely as their parents did when they were small. Jaana's mother, Minna's mother, Tiia's mother and Noora's parents compare the freedom of their own childhood with the limited space that their children have during the rest of the year in the city, constrained by the traffic and general insecurity.

The well-being of the child is reflected in the relationship with nature in a very deep sense. Maija's father tries to explain why nature and the countryside are so important for his daughter's play:

> When we were in Nauvo (in the archipelago) on the rocky shore, well, she had one little car with her then, but we were there a very long time and adults were with each other and Maija was there on the rocks, five hours, six hours, I don't know but a long time any way and there were only sticks and pebbles and then after the summer holidays I asked Maija, 'What was the best thing during the summer? What did you like best?' She said the rocky shore where there was not too much . . .
>
> Maybe it was the open seashore that influenced this remark. It is so different from her normal environment. When you move play from a child's bedroom to a seashore, or forest, the play takes on different meanings. There the terrain was changeable, dangerous and hard to move. I don't know if I'm over-interpreting, but maybe it was also fascinating for her because it is difficult to organise play in her bedroom, because there is so much of everything.

Yet, Maija's father does not know what Maija 'did' on the rocky shore. However, it was the best thing for her during the whole summer. The time Maija spent on the shore was seen by her parents as 'surplus time'. This means it was time which a child can spend the way she likes, for lovely inactivity, or play that carries her away. Apart from what Maija played – or did not play – her emotional well-being proves that a child does not always need programmes or toys in order to enjoy herself.

Max van Manen and Bas Levering (1996) emphasizes the importance of lovely inactivity, which is the state when children are all by themselves. This is the time when children find themselves and when even boredom raises new ideas and stimulates new action and imaginative ideas. Leisure time that is programmed by hobbies and television programmes does not promote the construction of the inner self.

Questions for reflective practice ▮

- How useful is it to know the culture for children?
- How can practitioners derive benefit from looking at play from different perspectives?
- How do children demonstrate their cultural competence and knowledge in their play?
- How do practitioners and parents show in practice that they appreciate play?

Further reading ▮

Bruce, T. (1991) *Time to Play in Early Childhood Education*. London: Hodder and Stoughton.

Bruce, T. (1996) *Helping Young Children to Play*. London: Hodder and Stoughton.

12

CHANGES IN CHILDREN'S PLAY CULTURE

Influences that are eroding children's play culture

Throughout this book we have seen:

- How changes in different types of children's play culture can be characterized.
- How these changes can be linked to changing child-rearing practices, influenced by the shift from a modern to a post modern atmosphere.
- How perceptions at the micro-level can be combined to give a general picture at a macro-level.
- How children's play culture looks now as compared with the 1950s.

Early childhood practice in different parts of the world has tended to be described using images of gardens and plant growth during the last hundred years or so. There is some evidence that children are being taken 'out of the garden'. We have looked at some of the ways this is happening:

- There are bare breasts on the TV screen and 'films that are too exciting' because of the crude violence in them.
- We see children release sexual tension through the 'dizziness' of body and language, and we see them act out stories such as the 'suicide on the playground slide' that imitate the adult relationships they see in drama on television.
- The weakened status of dolls indicates the shortening of childhood. Girls are reaching towards adulthood, balancing unsteadily on tiptoe like Barbie in her high-heeled shoes.

• The stereotypcial stories like those of Power Rangers and Biker Mice are becoming indispensable material for play, perhaps because stories with fights between good and evil are now hardly told in Finnish day-care centres. Maybe it is hard to tell such stories in a multi-valued and multi-valueless world. Maybe only commercial TV stories can unhesitatingly tell such polarized stories in a world where it is otherwise difficult to find global values presented through a fight between good and evil.

Television

Stephen Kline (1995) suggests that nowadays, commercial and stereo-typed television programmes with supplementary products have driven children out of the garden, so that children's play culture pulsates with rhythms defined by television.

The media environment today is dramatically different from that of the 1950s. As long as people lived without television, it was relatively easy to control the stories offered to children not yet able to read.

In the 1950s, the secrets of adult life were anticipated by children and revealed only gradually. What children learnt about adult life was based more on inner images than on graphic displays on TV. Now the world of some children – even 6-year-olds – is the world of one who has seen everything, a world where there are no secrets to arouse childlike curiosity.

Girls' interest in human relationships and boys' interest in action – which as such indicate the continuity of children's play culture – now manifest themselves in new ways. Girls may be seen reaching towards adulthood and the relationship between man and woman alongside the relationship between mother and child. Correspondingly boys tend to watch 'too exciting films'.

Children want to watch the same television programmes as adults, and naturally want the toys they see advertised in television. They want high status clothes or they may want to be the first to see a new Disney movie.

In a world where everyone has popular fashion objects, children constantly seek something that distinguishes them from the others. A collection of quality toys or visiting art exhibitions does not raise the status of a child among the peer group in the same way as having 'fashionable' toys.

Children have moved out of the garden

The metaphor 'out of the garden' also represents a concrete move-ment away from the home-based domestic backyards to the 'insti-tutional playground' of the day-care centres. In the previous chapter, we saw the parents of 6-year-olds reminisce about their own child-hood, when they had the freedom to wander much further than they will let their own children go. According to Kline (1995), there is much agreement that TV also explains the decline of street play, because it schedules children's lives and takes time away from out-door play. Children have moved indoors from the outside.

We saw in previous chapters that in the 1950s outdoor play took place in mixed age groups, which were less supervised by adults, whereas in early childhood setting today children typically play outdoors in the same age groups.

We can also see that children are being placed in situations where there is more open competition. Team games, with systematic, adult-directed rules, are replacing traditional games with rules, and we see less and less of children's own folklore in their play themes.

In many ways we see how uncertain child-rearing practices and the media environment of the today are reflected in the play of 6-year-olds so that they are being taken 'out of the garden' and towards the adults' world.

Sustained play of quality is instantly recognizable

Much play is brief and fragmented. Sustained play of great quality stands out when we see it. When it occurs, it indicates the high levels children can reach in their play.

The saying, 'to those who have shall be given' implying that those who have little will lose it, applies also to play. All of the 6-year-olds in this book are cherished by their families. Most are told fairytales and taken on excursions into the countryside or to museums. There are family weekends. These children are able to protect their own play space both at home and in the group setting. Although they might have moved 'out of the garden', they are still managing to keep hold of their own little piece of land which has something that is their own, and is out of the sight or understanding of adults. The survival of children's play culture – their little piece of land remains despite a fast changing world.

It would not be appropriate to sketch the general picture of child-ren's play culture using only one metaphor. Being 'pushed out of the garden', has an alternative, more positive feeling if we think of how children still have 'a little piece of land', even if it is not the secret garden of childhood.

We can list numerous ways in which children's play culture continues to flourish:

- Games played with adult rules have not totally taken over from the games from the children's own folklore, such as 'colour', 'mirror' or 'church rat', which we explored in previous chapters.
- 'Quarrel-solving rhymes' are used in new situations.
- Dizzy play continues to exist, and brings intense moments for sensible big sisters and wild little brothers or sisters.
- Children create new themes in their play, like 'the little fish that helped prevent pollution of the ocean'.
- The dominance of television programmes does not only impoverish children's play. Imaginative children, such as Tuomas, elaborate the stereotyped plots of Power Rangers, so that while imprisoned, the Power Rangers eat rye crisps and cereal rolls.
- The children who play 'Angel-princess and the egg of the flying horse' are using the structure of a classical fairy tale.
- The peer group is still an indispensable resource in constructing the play culture and a shared cultural competence is its solid base. Confident and imaginative players lead other children and invite them to share:
  - the victory of good over evil;
  - tender care
  - magic and make-believe
  - stories with a happy ending.
- Playing houses is still an important way of elaborating play themes.

Mika found a 'little piece of land' in his ice hockey play theme. During the long outings at the day-care centre, he usually plays 'ice-hockey-football' with other boys. To an outsider it just looks like ordinary football.

When he gets home, Mika makes a rink by turning a mat with roads and houses upside down. He darkens his room, takes a torch and lets the searchlight beam sweep the rink. He sings pieces of music and announces the players (ice hockey cards) as they enter the rink. At the start of a game Mika uses a rhyme he has made up: 'Who won the World Championship, Finland or Sweden, we are going to see it soon, one, two, out you go!'

The structure of Finnish society still offers time for sustained play, even for 6-year-olds. At the day-care centres, the long periods of time spent out of doors encourage this, although the argument for children spending time out of doors is more based on children's need to move and for fresh air, than on the importance of encouraging sustained play (Komiteamietintö 1980) (Figure 12.1). [Editor's note: Children in the UK are in primary education at this age, with less time for this kind of sustained play. Perhaps with the development of better transition into the first year of school, and as extended primary schools develop, there will be greater opportunity for children to keep hold of their little piece of land.]

An institutionalized childhood solves the problem of loneliness. According to research findings, being in a constant group develops the social skills of children (Strandell 1995). When Anu developed pneumonia and could not attend the day-care centre, she longed for Tiia, her friend. The peer group is indispensable for play. Several players are needed for most kinds of play. Group settings offer children friends to play with in abundance.

On the other hand, these children, with full-time working parents, play happily alone after a long day in a big group. Playing alone gives welcome privacy for a 6-year-old. For example, at home, Riikka transforms her most personal experiences into play. Here we see the distant father who 'does not like children'. At the day-care centre, when she and Miia play with the turtles, the imagined relationship between mother and child is handled in an extremely sensitive and nuanced way, but avoiding her deeply personal experiences.

Brian Sutton-Smith suggests that toys are linked with overcoming

Figure 12.1 Finnish 6-year-olds still have time to save worms during their day at the day-care centre.

loneliness. He argues that a toy given to a child soon changes into an adult demand for the child to 'Go to your room and play nicely' (1986: 23.). This does not fit with the child who has spent all day in a group setting, and enjoys the personal space of playing alone at home.

Indispensable play – finding ways of valuing play

It is impossible to totally reveal the secrets of play. The adult need to assess and evaluate play creates problems. How is it possible to appreciate a phenomenon that cannot be measured and rated? However, what adults manage to understand about play influences the space and energy adults give to encouraging children's play. There is a great variation in adults' attitudes towards play, even among the experts in early childhood education.

Friedrich Froebel (1826), the founder of the kindergarten, argued that play is the source of everything good, whereas Maria Montessori (1936) proclaims that children are not to play or eat sweets. The negative attitude of Montessori is consistent and implacable. She accuses Froebel of 'favouring the growth of symbolism' and finds toys as 'attractions offered to the mind that wanders in illusion'.

These questions recur time after time in the history of early childhood practice. Harriet Strandell (1994) wonders: 'Has the meaning of imagination been overestimated in the lives of children under school age?' and 'Are children forced to fantasize because they are not able to do so-called "real things"?' The beliefs of Strandell make one think of the Montessori philosophy that wonders whether maybe play is something marginal in the life of children and they take to it when there is nothing better available.

Real things are important, but the importance of real things does not diminish the meaning of play, because the two phenomena are different. The necessity to eat does not make rest less meaningful.

In play, it is also important to differentiate between the different kinds of play explored in this book, for example, dizzy play does not compensate for the commonly shared illusion of imitation and imaginative play. The thrill of destiny and chance does not compensate for the togetherness and momentous heroism of traditional competitive games with rules.

Strandell argues that because 'symbol and fantasy play seldom occur in their pure form', this is enough to indicate that play is of secondary importance to children (1995: 116). But this does not prove anything of the potential meaning of play. An analogy would be to suggest that if the results in learning language (English or Finnish) in schools are poor, we should conclude that learning language is not important. Instead, we ought to ask whether we leave too much to nature. Certainly, children learn to speak their mother tongue quite naturally, but this does not guarantee good language skills at school. Children play, too, but there is a difference between fragmentary play acting and deeply satisfying free flow play (Bruce 1991).

Strandell (1994) does not see fragmentation and momentary involvement in play as problems but rather sees them as a natural part of the postmodern way of living. For her, it is the adults' desire for clarity and order that is the problem. She sees the increasing disconnectedness of children's play as natural and inevitable. For her, it is not the result of conscious and unconscious action, and the pedagogical and cultural choices of adults. This interpretation supports the passivity typical of the uncertain child-rearing practices described in this book.

My own observations and research show that many a game ends before it has even started and very seldom does a game develop into an intense and long-lasting one. Many children don't experience the satisfaction of intense involvement in play. Unfortunately the constant outcry of my field diary, 'Where is the flow in play?' fits in many situations.

At times, when observing things, one can also identify the flow of play and 6-year-olds also reminisce about their play experiences in an intense way. Recalling the highlights of their best play is enjoyable. Laura asks: 'Do you remember how I was showering water like a waterfall?'

'Play is a threshold over which man crawls in order to enter a room where human life is lived.' This is how Lars-Erik Berg (1992) describes the essence of play.

To summarize:

- At an individual level, play belongs to growth.
- In shared play, a child can join the peer group as someone like the others, as a member of the group and as a leader.
- There is freedom of action in the roles of fantasy play and games with rules that are regulated by children themselves.
- Encouraging the child's imagination helps children to enjoy their childhood and become an adult who dares to see the world as it is and find new ways to live in the world.

The only thing we are able to say for certain about the future is the demand to support change and insecurity. So in order to manage these kinds of challenges as grown-ups, children need to be able to develop autonomy in order to become strong. One of the contributory factors of autonomy is imaginative competence, the ability to play, finding new ways in creative ways, and imagining other possible worlds.

What does the future of play look like?

Although adults might appreciate play in the way they talk about it, the status of play is ambiguous. The passivity of uncertain child-rearing practices and leaving children to themselves and expecting them to develop their own play are not enough.

According to Gunni Kärrby (1992) the most multifaceted and long-lasting play can be found in the early years settings where adults plan and run many-sided activities, and where the interaction between adults and children is given high priority and is multilayered.

It is unrealistically optimistic to believe that the ideal circumstances for play are created in the context of formal schooling. Mentioning the word play in the curriculum is not enough to guarantee quality play and games with numbers and letters do not compensate for sustained make-believe play. During break, children have time for clapping games but not for playing 'angel princess' or their other chosen themes.

Supporting children's play is more active than simply saying you believe it is important. When children's play culture is taken seriously, the conditions which make it flourish are carefully created. Children's play culture does not just happen naturally. Play needs time and space. It needs mental and material stimulation to be offered in abundance. Creating a rich play environment means creating a good learning environment for children. The themes discussed in this book will point the direction that practitioners should follow to make such an environment a reality.

Questions for reflective practice

- What will you do as a result of reading this book?
- Make an action plan which supports children in developing their play culture.
- Read about children's own play culture so that your thinking develops at a deeper level, and your practice wisdom is helped and supported.

Further reading ■

Bruce, T. (2004) *Developing Learning in Early Childhood*. London: Paul Chapman Publishing.

Gussin Paley, V. (1990) *The Boy Who Would Be a Helicopter*. Cambridge, MA: Harvard University Press.

Singer, D. and Singer, J. (1990) *The House of Make-Believe*. Cambridge, MA: Harvard University Press.

APPENDIX: INTERVIEWS

The transcribed interviews are in the author's possession. All the names in the interviews have been changed to code names. In addition, extra code names (Atte, Juulia, Minttu, Mira, Niklas and Toni) have been used on pp. 98–101.

Six-year-olds who were interviewed at home and at the day-care centre

Girls: Anu, Emilia, Emmi, Jaana, Juulia, Maija, Maria, Minna, Niina, Noora, Riikka, Sanna, Tiia; Boys: Antti, Jesse, Jonas, Joni, Jukka, Juuso, Kalle, Mika, Mikael, Oskari, Petri

Siblings

Eero, Jaana's big brother; Piia, Oskari's big sister; Sini, Emilia's big sister; Susanna, Noora's big sister; Tiina, Mika's little sister; Tommi, Sanna's big brother

Other children who are friends at the day-care centre or in the neighbourhood at home or other friends

Aapo, Akseli, Eetu, Elisa, Eveliina, Henna, Ilmari, Jere, Jenna, Joona, Jonna, Juho, Justus, Katariina, Lilli, Linda, Maarit, Mari, Miia, Miika, Mikko, Minttu, Olli, Pekka, Petteri, Riku, Saara, Sami, Samuli, Siiri, Tomi, Tomppa, Toni, Tuomas, Tuulia, Viltsu

Parents

Anu's mother and father, Emilia's mother and father, Emmi's mother, Jaana's mother, Maija's mother and father, Maria's mother, Minna's mother, Niina's mother, Noora's mother and father, Riikka's mother, Sanna's mother, Tiia's mother, Antti's father, Jesse's mother and father, Jonas's mother and father, Joni's mother and father, Jukka's mother, Juuso's mother, Kalle's mother, Mika's father, Mikael's mother, Oskari's mother and father, Petri's mother

Staff at the day-care centres

LTO means kindergarten teacher, LH means nursery nurse.

- Hilapieli: Aino, LH; Hanna, LH; Jarkko, LTO; Liisa, LTO; Marita, LTO; Mervi, LTO; Raili, LTO; Tarja, LTO; Ulla, LH.
- Kesäkumpu: Arja, LTO; Eija, LTO; Elina, LTO; Riitta, LTO
- Ulpukka: Helena, LTO; Pirjo, LH; Satu, LH; Sinikka, LTO

REFERENCES

Abrams, R. D. (1969) *Jump-Rope Rhymes: A Dictionary*. Austin, TX: University of Texas Press.

Alanen, L. (1992) *Modern Childhood? Exploring the 'Child Question' in Sociology*. Jyväskylä: Kasvatustieteiden tutkimuslaitos.

Bateson B. (1971) The Message 'This is Play'. In R. E. Herron and B. Sutton-Smith (eds) *Child's Play*. New York: John Wiley & Sons, Inc.

Bateson, G. ([1955] 1976) A theory of play and fantasy. In J. Bruner, A. Jolly and K. Sylva (eds) *Play: Its Role in Development and Evolution*. New York: Basic Books.

Beck, U. (1994) Reinventing politics: towards the theory of reflexive modernization. In U. Beck, A. Giddens and S. Lash (eds) *Reflexive Modernization: Politics, Tradition and Aesthetics in the Modern Social Order*. Cambridge: Polity Press.

Beck, U., Giddens, A. and Lash, S. (1994) *Reflexive Modernization: Politics, Tradition and Aesthetics in the Modern Social Order*. Cambridge: Polity Press.

Beck-Gernsheim, E. (1992) Everything for the child – for better or worse? In U. Björnberg (ed.) *European Parents in the 1990s: Contradictions and Comparisons*. New Brunswick and London: Transaction Publishers.

Berg, L-E. (1992) *Den lekande människan: En socialpsykologisk analys av lekandets dynamik*. Lund: Studentlitteratur.

Bergström, M. (1996) Aivofysiologinen näkökulma leikkiin ja esiopetukseen. In T. Jantunen and P. Rönnberg (eds) *Anna lapsen leikkiä*.

Bettelheim, B. (1975) *The Uses of Enchantment: The Meaning and Importance of Fairytales*. New York: Vintage Books.

Bjerrum-Nielsen, H. and Rudberg, M. (1991) *Historien om flickor och pojkar: Könssocialisation i ett utvecklingspsykologisk perspektiv*. Lund: Studentlitteratur.

Björnberg, U. (1992) Parenting in transition: an introduction and summary. In U. Björnberg (ed.) *European Parents in the 1990s; Contradictions and Comparisons*. New Brunswick and London: Transaction Publishers.

Bjurman, E-L. (1981) *Barn och barn: Om barns olika vardag*. Lund: Liber Läromedel.

Bruce, T. (1991) *Time to Play in Early Childhood Education*. London: Hodder & Stoughton.

Bruce, T. (1996) *Helping Young Children to Play*. London: Hodder and Stoughton.

Bruce, T. (2001) *Learning Through Play: Babies, Toddlers and the Foundation Years*. London: Hodder Arnold.

Bruce, T. (2004) *Developing Learning in Early Childhood*. London: Paul Chapman Publishing

Caillois, R. (1961) *Man. Play, and Games*. New York: The Free Press.

Cohen, D. ([1987] 1993) *The Development of Play*. New York: Routledge.

Cook-Gumperz, J. (1986) Caught in a web of words: some considerations on language socialization and language acquisition. In J. Cook-Gumperz, W. Corsaro and J. Streeck (eds) *Children's Worlds and Children's Language*. Berlin: Mouton de Gruyter.

Corsaro, W. (1985) *Friendship and Peer Culture in the Early Years*. Norwood, NJ: Ablex.

Corsaro, W. A. (1997) *The Sociology of Childhood*. Thousand Oaks, CA: Sage.

Csikszentmihalyi, M. (1975) *Beyond Boredom and Anxiety: The Experience of Play in Work and Games*. San Francisco: Jossey-Bass Publishers.

Danbolt, G. and Enerstvedt, Å. (1995) *Når voksenkultur og barns kultur mötes*. Oslo: Norsk Kulturråd.

Eide, B. (1989) Ett erkjennande forhold mellom barn og intervjuar – er det mogleg? In A. Lindth-Munter (ed.) *Barnintervjun som forskningsmetod*. Uppsala: Uppsala Universitet, pp. 93–112.

Ekrem, C. (1990) *Räkneramsor bland finlandssvenska barn*. Ekenäs: Svenska litteratursällskapet i Finland.

Elkind, D. (1994) *Ties That Stress: The New Family Imbalance*. Cambridge MA: Harvard University Press.

Enerstvedt, Å. (1982) *Tampen brenn: Norske barneleikar*. Oslo: Det Norske Samlaget.

Enerstvedt, Å. ([1971] 1984) *Kongen over gata: Oslobarns lek idag*. Oslo: Universitetsforlaget.

Finne, M. (1992) *Palikat, poikakärryt ja paperkukkaseppel: lastentarhojen leikkikulttuurista 20-luvulta 60-luvulle*. Helsinki: Finn Lectura.

Fiske, J. (1987) *Television Culture*. London: Routledge.

Frake, C. (1980) *Language and Cultural Descriptions*. Stanford, CA: Stanford University Press.

Francastel, P. (1995) Brueghel. Paris: Editions Hazan.

Fröbel, F. ([1826] 1982) *'Kommt, lasst uns unsern Kinder leben!': Aus dem pädagogischen Werk eines Menschenerziehers*. vol. 2. Berlin: Volk und Wissen. Volkseigener Verlag.

Frönes, I. (1994) Dimensions of childhood. In J. Qvortrup, M. Bardy, G. Sgritta and H. Wintersberger (eds), *Childhood Matters: Social Theory, Practice and Politics*. Avebury: European Centre Vienna.

Garvey, C. (1977) *Play*. Glasgow: Fontana.

Garvey, C. (1990) *Play*. rev. edn. Cambridge, MA: Harvard University Press.

Geertz, C. ([1973] 1993) *The Interpretations of Cultures*. London: Fontana Press.

Giddens, A. (1994) Life in a postmodern society. In U. Beck, A. Giddens and S. Lash (eds) *Reflexive Modernization: Politics, Tradition and Aesthetics in the Modern Social Order*. Cambridge: Polity Press.

Goldman, L. R. (1998) *Child's Play: Myth, Mimesis and Make-Believe*. New York and Oxford: Berg.

Gussin Paley, V. (1981) *Wally's Stories*. Cambridge, MA: Harvard University Press.

Gussin Paley, V. (1984) *Boys and Girls: Superheroes in the Doll Corner*. Chicago: University of Chicago Press.

Gussin Paley, V. (1986) *Mollie Is Three: Growing Up in School*. Chicago: University of Chicago Press.

Gussin Paley, V. (1990) *The Boy Who Would Be a Helicopter*. Cambridge, MA: Harvard University Press.

Hannerz, U. (1982) Delkulturerna och helheten. In U. Hannerz, R. Liljeström and O. Löfgren (eds) *Kultur och medvetande – en tvärvetenskaplig analys*. Angered: Akademilitteratur AB.

Hannerz, U., Liljeström, R. and Löfgren, O. (1982) *Kultur och medvetande – en tvärvetenskaplig analys*. Angered: Akademilitteratur AB.

Harris, J. R. (1998) *The Nurture Assumption: Why Children Turn Out the Way They Do*. New York: The Free Press.

Hautamäki, A. (2000) The matrix of relationships in the late modern family in the Nordic countries: a heaven in a heartless world, a disturbed nest or a secure base? In A. Hautamäki (ed.) *Emergent Trends in Early Childhood Education: Towards an Ecological and Psychohistorical Analysis of Quality*. Helsinki: University of Helsinki, Research Report no. 216 pp. 33–107.

Heggstad, K. M., Knudsen, I. M. and Trageton, A. (1994) *Fokus på lek:*

Estetikk, progresjon, kultur. Stord and Haugesund: Högskolen Stord/ Haugesund.

Helsingin Sanomat, 22 May 1997, Päiviscup oli taas lasten riemua.

Helsingin Sanomat, 28 Sept. 1997, Ei voi olla totta, vai voiko? Kotimaisen TV-sarjan on oltava uskottava jokaista pullaa ja purnukkaa myöten.

Helsingin Sanomat 15 Sept. 1998, Vaarin ja mummon iloa vailla vastuuta. Raisiossa päiväkoti ja vanhainkoti toimivat samoissa tiloissa.

Helsingin Sanomat 11 April 1999, Sarjat tunteita täynnä. Aiemmin TV-sarjoissa ei tapahtunut paljon mitään. Nyt pitää alkoholisoitua, pettää, kavaltaa tai kuolla ennen kuin katsojan sisällä liikahtaa.

Hoikkala, T. (1993) *Katoaako kasvatus, himmeneekö vanhemmuus? Aikuistumisen puhe ja kulttuurimallit.* Jyväskylä: Gaudeamus.

Holland, P. (2003) *We Don't Play with Guns Here: War, Weapons and Superhero Play in the Early Years.* Maidenhead: Open University Press.

Huizinga, J. ([1938] 1947) *Leikkivä ihminen: Yritys kulttuurin leikkiaineksen määrittelemiseen.* Porvoo-Helsinki: WSOY. (Originally *Homo Ludus.*)

Hujala, E., Puroila, A., Parrila-Haapakoski and Nivala, V. (1998) *Päivähoidosta varhaiskasvatukseen.* Jyväskylä: Varhaisvatus 90 Oy.

Huttunen, E. (1989) *Päivähoidon toimiva arki.* Suomen kaupunkiliitto.

Isaacs, S. ([1929] 1960) *The Nursery Years.* London: Routledge and Kegan Paul Ltd.

Isaacs, S. (1930) *Intellectual Growth in Young Children.* London: Routledge and Kegan Paul Ltd.

Isaacs, S. (1933) *Social Development in Young Children: A Study of Beginnings.* London: Routledge and Kegan Paul Ltd.

Itkonen, T. I. (1948) *Suomen lappalaiset II.* Porvoo: WSOY.

Kärrby, G. (1992) Lekandets plats i livet. Om lekens pedagogiska kraft (Riitta Kauppisen mukaeltu suomennos 'Juuret ovat puun aivot' – leikin kasvattava voima). In M. Riihelä and R. Kauppinen (eds) *Esiopetus linnunradalla.* STAKES Sosiaali- ja terveysalan tutkimus- ja kehittämiskeskus 1994. Raportteja 163.

Kitzinger, J. (1990) Who are you kidding? Children, power and the struggle against sexual abuse. In A. James and A. Prout (eds) *Constructing and Reconstructing Childhood. Contemporary Issues in the Sociology of Childhood.* London: The Falmers Press.

Kjörup, S. (1983) Barnen i bilderna. In C. Clausen (ed.) *Barnet blir barn.* Stockholm: Förlaget Barrikaden.

Kline, S. (1995) *Out of the Garden.* London and New York: Verso.

Komiteamietintö (1980) *Päivähoidon kasvatustavoitekomitean mietintö,* vol. 31.

Kotiliesi 24/1954, Ulla-nukke käy muotitalossa.

Kvale, S. (1996) *InterViews: An Introduction to Qualitative Research Interviewing.* London: Sage Publications.

Laevers, F. (1994) *The Innovative Project Experimental Education, 1976– 1994.* Research Centre for Early Childhood and Primary Education, Leuven: Katholieke Universiteit Leuven.

Lahikainen, A. R. and Kraav, I. (1996) Framing children's insecurity in postmodern society. In J. Hämäläinen, R. Vornanen and J. Laurinkoski (eds) *Social Work and Social Security in a Changing Society.* Augsburg: Maro Verlag.

Lancaster, P. (2005) Listening to Children. Maidenhead: Open University Press.

Lastentarha 8/1955, Henkilöitä.

Lastentarha 1/1995. Päiväkotipäiva on sociaalisuuden juhlaa.

Liliequist, M. (1993) Socialisation från vagga till graven. In B. Ehn (ed.) *Kultur och erfarenhet: Aktuella teman i svensk etnologi.* Stockholm: Carlssons.

Liuobart, M. (1997) New topics and characters of children's games in today's Russia. Paper presented to the Urban Childhood Conference, Trondheim, Norway, 9–12. June.

Magnusson, M. (1996) Vackert våld till salu. Teolsessal Brembeck, Helene & Barbo Johansson (eds): *Postmodern barndom.* Skrifter från Etnologiska föreningen i Västsverige 23, Göteborg 1996, 83–103.

Mäntynen, P. (1997) *Pikkulasten leikin edellytykset päiväkodissa.* Joensuu: Joensuun yliopistopaino.

Matthews, J. (2003) *Drawing and Painting: Children and Visual Representation.* 2nd edn. London: Paul Chapman Publishing.

Montessori, M. ([1936] 1998) *The Secret of Childhood.* London: Longmans, Green and Co.

Mouritsen, F. (1996) *Legekultur: Essays om børnekultur, leg och fortelling.* Gylling: Narayna Press.

Navarra, J. (1955) *The Development of Scientific Concepts in a Young Child: A Case Study.* New York: Teachers' College.

Olofsson, B. K. ([1991] 1993) *Varför leker inte barnen?* Stockholm: HLS förlag.

Olsson, G. (1956) Yhdessä leikkiminen. In A. Löfstedt and N. Bäckman (eds) *Äidin ja isän kirja.* Porvoo: WSOY, pp. 320–1.

Opie, I. and Opie P. ([1959] 1970a) *The Lore and Language of School Children.* Oxford: Oxford University Press.

Opie, I. and Opie, P. (1970b) *Children's Games in Street and Playground.* Oxford: Oxford University Press.

Opie, I. and Opie, P. (1970) *Children's Games with Things.* Oxford: Oxford University Press.

Opie, I. and Opie, P. (1985) *The Singing Game.* Oxford: Oxford University Press.

Opie, I. (1993) *The People in the Playground*. Oxford: Oxford University Press.

Ouvry, M. (2004) *Sounds Like Play*: Early Education.

Päivänsalo, P. (1952) *Yhteisöelämää lastentarhassa*. Helsinki: Suomen kasvatus-sosiologisen yhdistyksen julkaisuja No. 6.

Pascal, C. and Bertram, T. (1995) *Involvement and the Effective Early Learning Project: a collaborative venture. Jukaisussa An Exploration of the Concept or Involvement as an Indicator for Quality in Early Childhood Care and Education.* CIDREE, Consortium of Institutions for Development and Research in Education in Europe. Scottish Consultative Council on the Curriculum, 22–23.

Pennell, G. (1996) Why boys don't play Barbie: comparing children's and adult's perceptions of boy toys and girl toys. Paper presented to the International Toy Research Conference, Halmstad, Sweden, 17–22 June.

Piaget, J. ([1945] 1972) *Play, Dreams and Imitation*. New York: Norton.

Prout, A. and James, A. (1990) A new paradigm for the sociology of childhood? Provenance, promise and problems. In A. James and A. Prout *Constructing and Reconstructing Childhood: Contemporary Issues in the Sociological Study of Childhood.* London: The Falmers Press.

Pulkkinen, L. (1994) Millaista lastenkasvatusta nykytutkimus suosittelee? In J. Virkki (ed.) *Ydinperheestä yksilöllistyviin perheisiin.* Helsinki and Porvoo: WSOY.

Rasmussen, T. H. ([1992] 1993) *Den vilda leken*. Lund: Studentlitteratur.

Retter, H. (1979) *Spielzeug: Handbuch zur Geschichte und Pädagogik der Spielmittel.* Basel: Beltz.

Retter, H. (1998) *The future of children's play in a changing society and the task of educational theory.* Acta Universtatis Scientiarum Sosialium et artis Educardi Tallinnensis. A12.

Rönnberg, M. (1991) Televisio leikkinä. In K. Kauppila, S. Kuosmanen and M. Pallassalo (eds), *Rajaton ruutu: Kirjoituksia lapsista ja liikkuvasta kuvasta.* Mannerheimin lastensuojeluliitto.

Rönnberg, M. (1997) *TV är bra för barn*. Stockholm: Ekerlids Förlag.

Rossie, J-P. (1996) Toys in changing North African educational and sociocultural contexts. Paper presented to the International Toy Research Conference, Halmstad, Sweden, 17–22 June.

Ryle, G. (1971) *Collected Papers*. vol. II. *Collected Essays 1929–1968.* London: Hutchinson & Co.

Siltala, J. (1997) Das Ende des Homo Psychologicus. In P. Jüngst, K. Pfomm and H-J. Schulze-Göbel (eds) *Urbs et Regio*. Kassel: GhK, Kasseler Schriften zur Geographie und Planung.

Singer, D. G. and Singer, J. L. ([1990] 1992) *The House of Make-Believe*. Cambridge, MA: Harvard University Press.

Smilansky, S. (1968) *The Effects of Sociodramatic Play on Disadvantaged Preschool Children*. New York: John Wiley & Sons Ltd.

Strandell, H. (1994) *Sociala mötesplatser för barn: Aktivitetsprofiler och förhandlingskulturer på daghem*. Helsinki: Gaudeamus.

Strandell, H. (1995) *Päiväkoti lasten kohtaamispaikkana: Tutkimus päiväkodista sosiaalisten suhteiden kenttänä*. Tampere: Gaudeamus.

Sutton-Smith, B. (1976) *The Dialectics of Play*. Schorndorf: Verlag Hoffman.

Sutton-Smith, B. (1986) *Toys as Culture*. New York: Gardner Press.

Sutton-Smith, B. and Kelly-Byrne D. ([1984] 1986) The idealization of play. In P. K. Smith (ed.) *Play in Animals and Humans*. Oxford: Basil Blackwell.

Van Manen, M. and Levering, B. (1996) *Childhood's Secrets: Intimacy, Privacy and the Self Reconsidered*. New York: Teachers College, Columbia University.

Virtanen, L. (1970) *Antti, pantti, pakana: Kouluikäisten nykyperinne*. Porvoo: WSOY.

Vygotsky, L. S. ([1933] 1976) Play and its role in the mental development of the child. In J. Bruner, A. Jolly and K. Sylva (eds) *Play: Its Role in Development and Evolution*. New York: Basic Books. (Lecture given in Russian in 1933, published in English 1966.)

Ziehe, T. (1991) *Uusi nuoriso. Epätavanomaisen oppimisen puolustus. Tampere: Vastapaino. (Akuteos Plädoyer für ungewöhnliches Lernen.* 1982.

INDEX

1950s
  attitude to day-care 12–13
  backyard play 36, 37, 134
  dizzy play 102–3
  doll play 65–7, 68–9
  ideal of play 25
  make-believe play 72–3
  media environment 133
  outdoor play 134
  play fighting themes 90
  rhymes 48–9
  see also change
Abrams, R. D. 22
action play *see* play fighting
active play strategy 127–8
adults
  attitude to doll play 65–7
  dizzy play 22
  games devised by 37–9,
    40–1
  play framework 117
  relationship with children in
    studies 4, 6–7
  sensitivity to play 124
  see also parents; practitioners
adventure play 75–92
age
  and play 27, 35, 36, 64, 134
age segregation 36
agon see competition
Alanen, L. 14
alea see chance and destiny
'angels in the snow' 106
attitudes
  to day-care in 1950s 12–13
  to play 65–7, 137–8
authoritative parenthood 15
autonomy, and play 139

babies, portrayed in play 58
backgrounds, influence on play 62
backyard play 35, 36, 37, 49, 134
  see also tag games
'ball straddle tag' 32
Barbie dolls 69–70, 72, 122–3
Bateson, B.
Bateson, G. 18, 19, 96
Beck, U. 11, 41
Beck-Gernsheim, E. 12
Berg, L-E. 138
Bergström, M. 22
Bettelheim, B. 78
big sisters, portrayed in play 57–8
Biker Mice 133
  boys' use of story 86–7
  girls' use of story 89
Bjerrum-Nielsen, H. 91, 101, 111
Björnberg, U. 14
Bjurman, E-L. 37
black play 22
boundaries
  between children's and created
    culture 28–9
  in dizzy play 96
boy friends 72
boys
  fighting play 82–4, 86–8, 90, 91, 92
  girlish activities 115
  play style 26, 59–61, 91, 108–9, 112
  response to television 113–14, 133
brain, and play 22
Bruce, T. 18, 51, 128, 138
Brueghel, P. 25

Caillois, R. 1, 8, 15–16, 20, 22, 43
chance and destiny
  in games 43, 45–7, 111

play category 21
change
    in play culture 24–5, 36
    popularity of traditional games 37,
        125–6
    in society 10–13
    see also 1950s
chanting *see* rhymes
cheating, in chanting rhymes 46
child-rearing practices 15, 104,
        118–19, 125, 139
childhood, models 14
children
    competency 14
    marginalization 14
    relationships with parents 13–14
children's own games 37–8, 39
children's world, understanding of
        124–5
'church rat' game 30–2, 35
cognitive development, and play
        19–20
Cohen, D. 129
collective consciousness, in play 23
comedy, in play acting 62
communication, in make-believe
        play 51, 56–7
competency, of childhood 14
competition
    in adult devised games 38
    play category 21
    regulation by children 35
competitive play 30–42, 110–11
    differences from dizzy play 98
    see also rules
conflict, prevention through rhymes
        45
context, of play 24
control of situations, in games 34–5
Cook-Gumperz, J. 51
Corsaro, W. 4
countryside, outdoor play 130
Csikszentmihalyi, M. 18
cultural competence, in make-believe
        play 81
cultural context
    dizzy play 104
    play 24

cultural identity, and play 23
culture
    for children 26, 28, 38–9
    created by children 26–7, 28

Danbolt, G. 26
dark side, children investigating 91–2
day-care centres
    1950s attitude 12–13
    age segregation 36
    boys' play fighting 87
    group size 36
    outdoor play 135
day-care staff *see* practitioners
departure, stories of 75–6
destiny *see* chance and destiny
deuterolearning 19
disadvantaged children 37
dizziness, play category 22
dizzy play 94–105, 111, 129, 137
    in adults 20
    in competitive play 33–4
doll play 63–9, 132
    see also Barbie dolls

Ebenseser Kindergartens 102
Eide, B. 4
Ekrem, C. 28
Elkind, D. 15
emotional democracy 14
enemy role 86, 91–2
Enerstvedt, Å. 25, 26, 28
environment, for play 139
essentials for play 27
evil
    in make-believe play 79, 82–4, 85,
        86–7, 90, 91, 133
    television portrayal 133
evil role 86, 91–2

fairytale play 76–9
family
    changes in 15
    theme in make-believe play 52–6
fantasy play *see* make-believe play
fathers
    participation in play 129
    portrayed in play 58–9

fifties *see* 1950s
fight play *see* play fighting
films, source of adventure play 81
Finne, M. 67, 103
Fiske, J. 78
folklore *see* traditional
football, for young children 38–9
fragmentation, of play 138
Frake, C. 24
Francastel 25
freedom of action 11, 103, 122, 138
friendship, parents with children 119
Fröbel, F. 137
    principles 124
Frönes, I. 14

game-starting rhymes 43
games
    chance in 43, 45–7, 111
    children's own versus adults'
        devised 37–41
    competitive 30–3
    control of situations 34–5
Garvey, C. 19, 22, 24
Geertz, C. 5
gender differences
    affecting team games 39, 41
    hobbies 41
    and make-believe play 108–10, 112
    in play 26
    portrayed on TV 113–14
Giddens, A. 6, 14, 41
girls
    and boy friends 72
    boyish activities 115
    communication in make-believe
        play 56–7
    importance of relationships 57, 61,
        73, 113, 114, 133
    in play fighting 88–9, 90
    play style 26, 56–9, 61, 90, 91,
        109–10, 112
    response to television 114–15, 133
    sexual word play 98–101
    version of *Biker Mice* 89
Goldman, L. R. 23
good and evil 82–4, 85, 86–7, 90, 91
    television portrayal 133

group discussions, for book 7
group play
    and competition 32
    make-believe play 78
    need for 136
    and older children 27
    see also peer group play
guns 24, 88, 122–3
Gussin Paley, V. 4, 26

Hannerz, U. 23, 27
Harris, J. R. 39, 111
Hautamäki, A. 15
Heggstad, K. M. 128
historic events, and changes in play
    24
hobbies 37
    encouragement by parents
        119–20
    gender differences 41
Hoikkala, Tommi 13, 14
Holland, P. 87, 123
home
    parents support for play 128–31
    play facilities 35–6
Huizinga, J. 17, 18
human relationships, in girls' play
    57, 61, 73, 113, 114, 133

'ice-hockey-football' game 34
identity
    boys 92, 114
    and change 11
ilinx see dizziness; dizzy play
imaginative play 138
imitation
    in competitive play 34
    in make-believe play 52
    play category 21–2
inactivity, importance of 131
independence, make-believe play 57
influences, on children's play 10, *11*,
    132–7
interruption culture 127
interviews, for book 5–7
invisible characters, in fighting play
    87
involvement in play 126–7

Isaacs, S. 2, 22
Itkonen, T. I. 24

James, A. 14

Kärrby, G. 139
Kelly-Burne, D. 104
Ken (boy Barbie) 69–70
kirkonrotta game 30–2, 35
'kiss tag' 33, 111
Kitzinger, J. 14
Kjörup, S. 25
Kline, S. 37, 133, 134
knowledge, use in fantasy play 80
Komiteamietintö 136
kotikatu (television soap) 115
Kraav, I. 114
Kvale, S. 5

Lahikainen, A. R. 114, 115
Lancaster, P. 4
Lash, C. 41
learning by heart, rhymes 49
learning through play 19
Levering, B. 124
Lieliequist, M. 38
Liliequist, M. 38
Liuobart, M. 24
lost children, make-believe play
    55–6, 75–6
love, represented in play 71–2
luck *see* chance and destiny

Magnusson, M. 90
make-believe play 21–2, 23, 51–73
    adventure play 75–92
    in competitive play 34
    cultural competence 81
    and gender 108–10, 112
    use of knowledge 80
    using rhymes for casting 43–4, 45,
        47
    support in day-care centres 127
male role, in play 109
Mäntynen, Pirkko 127
map-maker model, play 23–4
marginalization, of children 14
masculine role 109

media, effect on play 133
media play 85
mimicry see imitation
'mirror and colour' game 32
mixed age ranges 35, 36, 134
models
    child-rearing 15
    childhood 14
    map-maker for play 23–4
modern play, positive aspects 135
modernism 11
Montessori, M. 137
'Moomin tag' 33
Moomins, and child-rearing practices
    118
mothers
    participation in play 128–9
    portrayed in play 52–6, 57
Mouritsen, F. 25, 27

narratives, of children's play 5
nature, interaction with 129–30
news items, in play 126
'noisy time', in 1950s 102–3
nursery nurses *see* practitioners

observation, of play 7, 124
older children, in group play 27
Olofsson, B. K. 67
Olsson, G. 103
Opie, I. 1, 22, 28, 37
Opie, P. 1, 22, 28, 37
originality, of play scenarios 81
'out of the garden' phenomenon
    134
outdoor play
    in countryside 130
    in day-care centres 135
    loss of 134

Päivänsalo, P. 68
parenting 15, 104, 118–19, 125,
    139
parents
    encouragement of hobbies 119–20
    friendship with children 119
    interviews for book 6
    participation in play 102, 129

relationships with children 13–14,
  119
imitation by children 55–6
rough and tumble play 97
support for play 128–31
see also adults
passive attitude, to play 127, 138,
  139
peer group play 135, 138
  see also group play
Pennell, G. 64
Peter Rabbit, use of story 82
physical play *see* competitive play;
  dizzy play
Piaget, J. 19
play
  changes in 24–5, 36
  classification 8, 20–3, 106–7
  constancy 25
  cultural context 24
  definitions 17–18
  fragmentation 138
  nature of 18–20
  effect of societal change 10–11
  support 120–1, 128–31
  see also group play; peer group play
play acting 22, 23
  use of cultural material 28
  see also adventure play;
    competitive play; make-believe
play environment 139
play fighting 82–92
  dizzy play 95–7
play scenarios *see* scenarios
playgrounds, 1950s 103
playing houses 61–2
politics, effect of collapse on
  children's play 24
pornography, access to 99–100
post-war period *see* 1950s
postmodernism 11
power
  boys' view of 114
  using rhymes to exclude players
    46
Power Rangers 133
  adult attitude towards 92
  boys' use of story 83–4

practitioners
  intervention in play 122, 124,
    126
  interviews for book 6–7
  support of play 120–2
  response to wandering children
    125–6
  see also adults
'President tag' 33
props, for make-believe play 82
Prout, A. 14
Pulkkinen, L. 15
'pyllyttely' 96

quality, in play 134
quarrel prevention rhymes 45

racism, in fictional character
  portrayal 90–1
Rasmussen, T. H. 128
real-life
  in make-believe play 79
  reflection in play 61–2
relationships
  of adults with children in study 4,
    6–7
  children with nature 129–30
  importance in girls' play 57, 61, 73,
    113, 114, 133
  between parents and children
    13–14, 119
  portrayed in make-believe play
    55–6, 69–72
Retter, H. 24
revival, in make-believe play 79–80
rhymes
  learning 47–8, 49
  for preventing conflict 45
  for selecting players 43–4, 45,
    47
  traditional 44–5, 107
  uses of 45–7
role models, identification with
  116
Rönnberg, M. 85, 92, 115–16
Rossie, J-P. 24
rough and tumble play 97
Rudberg, M. 91, 101, 111

rules
and competition 21
in play 19
see also competitive play
Ryle, G. 5

scenarios
adventure play 76–9
originality 81
scripts 84–5
suicide 70–1
scripts, for play scenarios 84–5
seashore, play 130
sense of identity *see* identity
sensitivity to children's play 124
sex themes
in play 98–101, 104–5
on television 115
sexual word play, in dizzy play
98–101
shared scenarios, for play 77–8
sharing toys, rhymes 46
signals, indicating play 18
Siltala, J. 127
Singer, D. G. 20
Singer, J. L. 20
sisters, portrayed in play 57–8
Smilansky, S. 21
soaps, television 114–15
society, impact of change 10–13,
11
solo play 61, 67–8, 82, 136
status, ownership of fashionable toys
133
stereotyping, in fictional characters
90
Strandell, H. 4, 14, 127, 136, 137,
138
suicide, play scenario 70–1
Sutton-Smith, B. 22, 104, 136–7
swivelling 94
swords 24, 88, 122–3

tag games 30–3, 110–11
see also backyard play
'tar pot' game 32
teachers *see* practitioners
team games 40–1

television
adults watching children's
programmes 124–5
gendered programmes 113–14
and ideas for play 81–2, 87, 126,
133
effect on play 37, 73, 132, 133
sex themes 99–100, 105, 115
violence 114
tolerance, in children's own games
39
toys
and gender 113
sharing using rhymes 46
and solo play 136–7
and status 133
TV characters in day-care centres
122–3
traditional games 41–2, 106–7
change in popularity 37, 125–6
traditional rhymes 44–5, 48–9, 107
traditions, in play 25
Tuulia 66

unpredictability, of play 19
unproductiveness, of play 19, 20
unrestrained play, dizzy play 96
USSR, effect of collapse on children's
play 24

Van Manen, M. 124, 131
violence, on TV 114
Virtanen, L. 25, 28, 43, 49
vital family 15
voluntary nature of play 18
Vygotsky, Lev S. 19–20

'wandering' children 126–7
war toys *see* weapons play
weapons play 24, 88, 122–3
weddings, in play 69–70
white play 22
'wild dog' play 95–6, 98
working mothers, portrayed in play
57

Ziehe, T. 11
zone of proximal development 20